The Enchanted Cat

The Enchanted Cat

John Richard Stephens

Prima Publishing & Communications
P.O. Box 1260 EC
Rocklin, CA 95677
(916) 624-5718

The author wishes to express special appreciation to Frank and Mary Beth DiVito, Bill and Noreen Hilden, and Marty Goeller, all of whom love cats.

Typography by Janet Hansen and Solotype
Copyediting by Jerilyn Emori
Production by Rosaleen Bertolino, Bookman Productions
Interior Design by Hal Lockwood and Judith Levinson
Cover design by The Dunlavey Studio

Prima Publishing & Communications
Rocklin, CA

Library of Congress Cataloging-in-Publication Data

The enchanted cat / [edited] by John Richard Stephens.
p. cm.
Includes index.
ISBN 1-55958-045-3 : $12.95
1. Cats—Literary collections. 2. Cats in art.
I. Stephens.
John Richard.
PN6071.C3E5 1990 90-8872
808.8″036—dc20 CIP

90 91 92 93 RRD 10 9 8 7 6 5 4 3 2 1

Printed in the United States of America

Acknowledgments in the credits on pages 233–237 constitute an extension of the copyright page.

This book was written for
and is dedicated to Martha Anne Stephens

A Spring Day

Sun on the long grass
Butterflies dance in the air
Chased by a kitten.

Haiku by John Richard Stephens

How to Order:

Quantity discounts are available from Prima Publishing & Communications, Post Office Box 1260EC, Rocklin, CA 95677; telephone (916) 624-5718. On your letterhead include information concerning the intended use of the books and the number of books you wish to purchase.

For your further enjoyment, this book is available in an audio cassette. Please contact Audio Renaissance at: 5858 Wilshire Boulevard, Suite 205, Los Angeles, CA 90036 (213) 939-1840.

U.S. Bookstores and Libraries: Please submit all orders to St. Martin's Press, 175 Fifth Avenue, New York, NY 10010; telephone (212) 674-5151.

Contents

C H A P T E R 1

Waiting in the Sunlight

Ye shall not possess any beast, my dear sisters, except only a cat.

The Ancren Riewle (Nun's Rule), England, 1205.

Our perfect companions never have fewer than four feet.

Colette (1873–1954).

As we begin our exploration, let us start within our paradigm—the world of the cat as we know it. In this first chapter we'll explore friendships with cats and why we're attracted to them. Later we'll move away from the world of the familiar, away from the world of our daily patterns, into the abyss of the supernatural and the unknown.

Cats lack our preconceived notions of what the world is all about. Oblivious to the cares, worries, and desires that plague us, they sit back and watch the world, observing without making judgments, rather like small furry Buddhas. Maybe it's this Zen outlook that attracts us to cats. They accept us as we are, without passing judgment.

Still, the friendship of a cat is not as freely given as, say, that of a dog. A cat must be won over, and her friendship, once obtained, must not be neglected or she may move on to someone more deserving of her affections. It's this that makes her friendship valuable. If we are devoted to her, she will reward us with loyalty that rivals that of a dog.

There once was a famous Arabian stallion who was close friends with a cat. In 1753, when the horse died, the cat sat upon him until he was buried. The cat then crept slowly away and wasn't seen again until her body was found in a hayloft. Surely it is this undying friendship, so rarely found in other animals, that has attracted people to cats over the centuries.

Cat in the Rain

ERNEST HEMINGWAY, from *In Our Time*, 1925. American novelist and journalist.

Le chat, Pablo Picasso, 1942. Spanish painter and sculptor.

There were only two Americans stopping at the hotel. They did not know any of the people they passed on the stairs on their way to and from their room. Their room was on the second floor facing the sea. It also faced the public garden and the war monument. There were big palms and green benches in the public garden. In the good weather there was always an artist with his easel. Artists liked the way the palms grew and the bright colors of the hotels facing the gardens and the sea. Italians came from a long way off to look up at the war monument. It was made of bronze and glistened in the rain. It was raining. The rain dripped from the palm trees. Water stood in pools on the gravel paths. The sea broke in a long line in the rain and slipped back down the beach to come up and break again in a long line in the rain. The motor cars were gone from the square by the war monument. Across the square in the doorway of the cafe a waiter stood looking out at the empty square.

The American wife stood at the window looking out. Outside right under their window a cat was crouched under one of the dripping green tables. The cat was trying to make herself so compact that she would not be dripped on.

"I'm going down and get that kitty," the American wife said.

"I'll do it," her husband offered from the bed.

"No, I'll get it. The poor kitty out trying to keep dry under a table."

The husband went on reading, lying propped up with the two pillows at the foot of the bed.

"Don't get wet," he said.

The wife went downstairs and the hotel owner stood up and bowed to her as she passed the office. His desk was at the far end of the office. He was an old man and very tall.

"Il piove," the wife said. She liked the hotel-keeper.

"Si, si, Signora, Brutto tempo. It's very bad weather."

He stood behind his desk in the far end of the dim room. The wife liked him. She liked the deadly serious way he received any complaints. She liked his dignity. She liked the way he wanted to serve her. She liked the way he felt about being a hotel-keeper. She liked his old, heavy face and big hands.

Liking him she opened the door and looked out. It was raining harder. A man in a rubber cape was crossing the empty square to the cafe. The cat would be around to the right. Perhaps she could go along under the eaves. As she stood in the doorway an umbrella opened behind her. It was the maid who looked after their room.

"You must not get wet," she smiled, speaking Italian. Of course, the hotel-keeper had sent her.

With the maid holding the umbrella over her, she walked along the gravel path until she was under their window. The table was there, washed bright green in the rain, but the cat was gone. She was suddenly disappointed. The maid looked up at her.

"Ha perduto qualque cosa, Signora?"

"There was a cat," said the American girl.

"A cat?"

"Si, il gatto."

"A cat?" the maid laughed. "A cat in the rain?"

"Yes," she said, "under the table." Then, "Oh, I wanted it so much. I wanted a kitty."

When she talked English the maid's face tightened.

"Come, Signora," she said. "We must get back inside. You will be wet."

"I suppose so," said the American girl.

They went back along the gravel path and passed in the door. The maid stayed outside to close the umbrella. As the American girl passed the office, the padrone bowed from his desk. Something felt very small and tight inside the girl. The padrone made her feel very small and at the same time really important. She had

The Big Cat, Conelis Vischer (1610–1670).

a momentary feeling of being of supreme importance. She went on up the stairs. She opened the door of the room. George was on the bed, reading.

"Did you get the cat?" he asked, putting the book down.

"It was gone."

"Wonder where it went to," he said, resting his eyes from reading.

She sat down on the bed.

"I wanted it so much," she said. "I don't know why I wanted it so much. I wanted that poor kitty. It isn't any fun to be a poor kitty out in the rain."

George was reading again.

She went over and sat in front of the mirror of the dressing table looking at herself with the hand glass. She studied her profile, first one side and then the other. Then she studied the back of her head and her neck.

"Don't you think it would be a good idea if I let my hair grow out?" she asked, looking at her profile again.

George looked up and saw the back of her neck, clipped close like a boy's.

"I like it the way it is."

"I get so tired of it," she said. "I get so tired of looking like a boy."

George shifted his position in the bed. He hadn't looked away from her since she started to speak.

"You look pretty darn nice," he said.

She laid the mirror down on the dresser and went over to the window and looked out. It was getting dark.

"I want to pull my hair back tight and smooth and make a big knot at the back that I can feel," she said. "I want to have a kitty to sit on my lap and purr when I stroke her."

"Yeah?" George said from the bed.

"And I want to eat at a table with my own silver and I want candles. And I want it to be spring and I want to brush my hair out in front of a mirror and I want a kitty and I want some new clothes."

"Oh, shut up and get something to read," George said. He was reading again.

His wife was looking out of the window. It was quite dark now and still raining in the palm trees.

"Anyway, I want a cat," she said, "I want a cat. I want a cat now. If I can't have long hair or any fun, I can have a cat."

George was not listening. He was reading his book. His wife looked out of the window where the light had come on in the square.

Someone knocked at the door.

"Avanti," George said. He looked up from his book.

In the doorway stood the maid. She held a big tortoise-shell cat pressed tight against her and swung down against her body.

"Excuse me," she said, "the padrone asked me to bring this for the Signora."

La Ménagerie intime (excerpt)

THÉOPHILE GAUTIER, 1850. French poet, critic, and novelist.

It is no easy task to win the friendship of a cat. He is a philosopher, sedate, tranquil, a creature of habit, a lover of decency and order. He does not bestow his regard lightly, and, though he may consent to be your companion, he will never be your slave. Even in his most affectionate moods he preserves his freedom, and refuses a servile obedience. But once gain his confidence, and he is a friend for life. He shares your hours of work, of solitude, of melancholy. He spends whole evenings on your knee, purring and dozing, content with your silence, and spurning for your sake the society of his kind.

Paul Audra, 1888. French artist.

Our Cats and All about Them (excerpt)

HARRISON WEIR, 1889. British author and illustrator.

The cat, like many other animals, will often form singular attachments. One would sit in my horse's manger and purr and rub against his nose, which undoubtedly the horse enjoyed, for he would frequently turn his head purposely to be so treated. One went as consort with a Dorking cock; another took a great liking to my collie, Rover; another loved Lina, the cow; while another would cosset up close to a sitting hen, and allowed the fresh-hatched chickens to seek warmth by creeping under her. Again, they will rear other animals such as rats, squirrels, rabbits, puppies, hedgehogs; and, when motherly inclined, will take to almost anything, even to a young pigeon.

Unknown artist, 1800s.

The Innocents Abroad (excerpt)

MARK TWAIN, 1869, while visiting the Zoological Gardens at Marseilles, France. American writer.

The boon companion of the colossal elephant was a common cat! This cat had a fashion of climbing up the elephant's hind legs, and roosting on his back. She would sit up there, with her paws curved under her breast, and sleep in the sun half the afternoon. It used to annoy the elephant at first and he would reach up and take her down, but she would go aft and climb up again. She persisted until she finally conquered the elephant's prejudices, and now they are inseparable friends. The cat plays about her comrade's forefeet or his trunk often, until dogs approach, and then she goes aloft in danger. The elephant has annihilated several dogs lately, that pressed his companion too closely.

Mark Twain and one of his many cats.

Love and Strength, Angelo Graf von Courten, ca. 1894.

(Untitled)

APION, 1st century A.D. Greek grammarian and commentator who claimed to be an eyewitness to this story.

One day, that at Rome they entertained the people with the fighting of several strange beasts, and principally of lions of an unusual size, there was one amongst the rest who, by his furious deportment, by the strength and largeness of his limbs, and by his loud and dreadful roaring, attracted the eyes of all the spectators. Amongst the other slaves, that were presented to the people in this combat of beasts, there was one Androclus, of Dacia, belonging to a Roman lord of consular dignity. This lion, having seen him at a distance, first made a sudden stop, as it were, in a wondering posture, and then softly approached nearer in a gentle and peaceable manner, as if it were to enter into acquaintance with him; this being done, and being now assured of what he sought, he began to wag his tail, as dogs do when they flatter their master and to kiss and lick the hands and thighs of the poor wretch, who was beside himself and almost dead with fear. Androclus having, by this kindness of the lion, a little come to himself, and having taken so much heart as to consider and recognize him, it was a singular pleasure to see the joy and caresses that passed betwixt them. At which the people breaking into loud acclamations of joy, the emperor caused the slave to be called, to know from him the cause of so strange an event. He thereupon told him a new and very wonderful story: my master, said he, being proconsul in Africa, I was constrained by his severity and cruel usage, being daily beaten, to steal from him and to run away. And to hide myself securely from a person of so great authority in the province, I thought it my best way to fly to the solitudes, sands, and uninhabitable parts of that country, resolved, in case the means of supporting life should fail me, to make some shift or other to kill myself. The sun being excessively hot at noon, and the heat intolerable, I found a retired and almost inaccessible cave, and went into it. Soon after there came in to me this lion with one foot wounded and bloody, complaining and groaning with the pain he endured: at his coming I was exceedingly afraid, but he having espied me hid in a corner of his den, came gently to me, holding out and showing me his wounded foot, as if he demanded my assistance in his distress. I then drew out a great splinter he had got there, and growing a little more familiar with him, squeezing the wound, thrust out the dirt and gravel that he had got into it, wiped and cleansed it as well as I could. He, finding himself something better and much eased of his pain, lay down to repose, and presently fell asleep with his foot in my hand. From that time forward, he and I lived together in this cave three whole years, upon the same diet; for of the beasts that he killed in hunting he always brought me the best pieces, which I roasted in the sun for want of fire, and so ate them. At last growing weary of this wild and brutish life, the lion being one day gone abroad to hunt for our ordinary provision, I escaped from thence, and the third day after was taken by the soldiers, who brought me from Africa to this city to my master, who presently condemned me to die, and to be exposed to the wild beasts. Now, by what I see, this lion was also taken soon after, who would now recompense me for the benefit and cure that he had received at my hands. This is the story that Androclus told the emperor, which he also conveyed from hand to hand to the people: wherefore at the universal request, he was absolved from his sentence and set at liberty; and the lion was, by order of the people, presented to him. We afterwards saw, Androclus leading this lion, in nothing but a small leash, from tavern to tavern at Rome, and receiving what money everybody would give him, the lion being so gentle, as to suffer himself to be covered with the flowers that the people threw upon him.

Pangur Bán

IRISH MONK, 8th century. Written in Gaelic on a copy of St. John's Epistles at Reichenau, the monastery of Corinthia. Pangur Bán means "white cat."

I and Pangur Bán, my cat,
'Tis a like task we are at;
Hunting mice is his delight,
Hunting words I sit all night.

Better far than praise of men
'Tis to sit with book and pen;
Pangur bears me no ill-will,
He too plies his simple skill.

'Tis a merry thing to see
At our tasks how glad are we,
When at home we sit and find
Entertainment to our mind.

Oftentimes a mouse will stray
In the hero Pangur's way;
Oftentimes my keen thought set
Takes a meaning in its net.

'Gainst the wall he sets his eye
Full and fierce and sharp and sly;
'Gainst the wall of knowledge I
All my little wisdom try.

When a mouse darts from its den,
Oh, how glad is Pangur then!
Oh, what gladness do I prove
When I solve the doubts I love!

The White Cat, Meredith Nugent.

So in peace our task we ply,
Pangur Bán—my cat—and I;
In our arts we find our bliss,
I have mine and he has his.

Practice every day has made
Pangur perfect in his trade;
I get wisdom day and night
Turning darkness into light.

Hungry Master and Hungry Cat

ABU SHAMAQMAQ, ca. A.D. 770. Translated from Arabic.

Cat, Alberto Giacometti (1901–1966), Swiss sculptor.

When my house was bare of skins and pots of meal,
after it had been inhabited, not empty, full of folk and richly
prosperous,
I see the mice avoid my house, retiring to the governor's palace.
The flies have called for a move, whether their wings are clipped
or whole.
The cat stayed a year in the house and did not see a mouse
shaking its head at hunger, at a life full of pain and spite.
When I saw the pained downcast head, the heat in the belly, I said,
"Patience; you are the best cat my eyes ever saw in a ward."
He said, "I have no patience. How can I stay in a desert like the
belly of a she ass?"
I said, "Go in peace to a hotel where travellers are many and much
trade,
Even if the spider spins in my wine jar, in the jug, and the pot."

Rendezvous

PAUL GALLICO, from *Honorable Cat*, 1972. American poet.

I am waiting for my mistress to come home from school.
She is nine years old,
Accounted by us as still a kitten.
She is gone from early morn
Until the sun is low.
I miss her.
When she is in the house
My purr throbs in my throat.
When she is gone
I go to her empty room
And lie on something
That is hers,
And wait until I know
She will be coming down the street,
Carrying her satchel,
Her braids swinging as she skips.
Sometimes when she walks with friends
She will ignore me and forget
That I am there.
I will come down from where I perch
And follow her,
My tail her banner,
My song of joy her music,
For all that matters is
That she is home again.
Or she will pluck me from the wall
And hold me to her lips and talk to me
And I could die of love.
She plays with me as though I were a toy,
Clothed in doll's dresses,
Or perched in the high chair
That once was hers.

By François Drouais (1727–1775).

She lifts me by tender legs,
Holds me to her across my middle,
Or wears me like a shawl across her shoulders;
Cradles me in her arms
Pretending I am her kitten,
And sings me lullabies.
I know her smells,
Her hair, her apron and her ribbons,

The orange and the sticky sweet she had for lunch
Still on her fingers and her clothes.
Her shrill voice sometimes hurts my ears;
Her careless feet have often trod my tail;
Her scoldings and her storms of anger
I endure.
But when she weeps I leap into her lap
To try to comfort her.
I lick the salt tears from her face,
Feel the damp cheek press into my fur
And share her misery,
Until once more her laughter comes.
She doesn't laugh, she gurgles with delight,
A sound mysterious as my purr
And she will snatch me up
And hug me fiercely so that I must cry out.
Her voice then tells me she is sorry,
And we are friends.

I have no register for Time,
Moonrise and sunrise only.
I cannot count the passage of the days,
Or solve the mysteries of clocks,
Minutes and seconds
A beginning or an end.
And yet, each day within me
There strikes the hour of her return.
I know,
And I am here to meet her.

A Poet's Lamentation for the Loss of his Cat (excerpt)

JOSEPH GREEN, 1733. American poet and distiller.

Henry Wriothesley, 3d Earl of Southampton, while in the Tower of London, attributed to John de Critz, 1603. A patron of William Shakespeare, the earl was sentenced to death by Queen Elizabeth I for trying to depose the queen's councils and was later pardoned by King James I. In 1607 he helped finance John Smith's settlement at Jamestown, the first permanent English settlement in America.

Whene'er I felt my towering fancy fail,
I stroked her head, her ears, her tail,
And, as I stroked, improved my dying song
From the sweet notes of her melodious tongue.
Her purrs and mews so evenly kept time,
She purred in metre and she mewed in rhyme.

Sir Walter Scott and his cat.

Bravo

PHILIP DACEY, from *Seems* magazine, 1989. American poet and professor. Bravo is his Siamese cat.

O, what a fortuitous choice,
Bravo as the name for my cat!
For now when I call him in
I face the woods and cry, Bravo!
or the creek near the house and cry, Bravo!
or the meadow of wildflowers and cry, Bravo!
Wherever I turn, I cry, Bravo!
Whatever I see, I cry, Bravo!
And the place that encircles me,
that I bravo and bravo and bravo,
like an actor bowing and taking
the thunderous love from the darkness
who steps forward to give the love back,
all applause for those who applaud him—
that place gives bravo for bravos,
as if pleased to acknowledge my cries
that acknowledge how great is the show
from horizon around to horizon,
sky, stream, and ground, for out
of the shadows and springing, all paws,
comes—Bravo!—Bravo the cat.

Chinese, Ching Dynasty (1644–1912).

Title Unknown

CHARLES BAUDELAIRE (1821–1867). French poet.

Come, lovely cat, and rest upon my heart,
    And let my gaze dive in the cold
Live pools of thine enchanted eyes that dart
    Metallic rays of green and gold.

My fascinated hands caress at leisure
    Thy head and supple back, and when
Thy soft electric body fills with pleasure
    My thrilled and drunken fingers, then

Thou changest to my woman; for her glance,
    Like thine, most lovable of creatures,
Is icy, deep, and cleaving as a lance.

    And round her hair and sphinx-like features
And round her dusky form float, vaguely blent,
    A subtle air and dangerous scent.

Juno

HARRIET BEECHER STOWE (1811–1896), author of *Uncle Tom's Cabin* (1854), American author. The rear of her property adjoined Mark Twain's.

The most beautiful and best trained cat I ever knew was named Juno, and was brought up by a lady who was so wise in all that related to the care and management of animals, that she might be quoted as authority on all points of their nurture and breeding; and Juno, carefully trained by such a mistress, was a standing example of the virtues which may be formed in a cat by careful education.

Never was Juno known to be out of place, to take her nap elsewhere than on her own appointed cushion, to be absent at meal-

Cat and hearth belonging to John Greenleaf Whittier, American poet, during the winter he wrote "Snow-Bound" (1866).

times, or, when the most tempting dainties were in her power, to anticipate the proper time by jumping on the table to help herself.

In all her personal habits Juno was of a neatness unparalleled in cat history. The parlor of her mistress was always of a waxen and spotless cleanness, and Juno would have died sooner than violate its sanctity by any impropriety. She was a skillful mouser, and her sleek, glossy sides were a sufficient refutation of the absurd notion that a cat must be starved into a display of her accomplishments. Every rat, mouse, or ground mole that she caught was brought in and laid at the feet of her mistress for approbation. But on one point her mind was dark. She could never be made to comprehend the great difference between fur and feathers, nor see why her mistress should gravely reprove her when she brought in a bird, and warmly commend when she captured a mouse.

After a while a little dog named Pero, with whom Juno had struck up a friendship, got into the habit of coming to her mistress's apartment at the hours when her modest meals were served, on which occasions Pero thought it would be a good idea to invite himself to make a third. He had a nice little trick of making himself amiable, by sitting up on his haunches, and making little begging gestures with his two fore-paws,—which so much pleased his hostess that sometimes he was fed before Juno. Juno observed this in silence for some time; but at last a bright idea struck her, and, gravely rearing up on her haunches, she imitated Pero's gestures with her fore-paws. Of course this carried the day, and secured her position.

Cats are often said to have no heart,—to be attached to places, but incapable of warm personal affection. It was reserved for Juno by her sad end to refute this slander on her race. Her mistress was obliged to leave her quiet home, and go to live in a neighboring city; so she gave Juno to the good lady who inhabited the other part of the house.

But no attentions or care on the part of her new mistress could banish from Juno's mind the friend she had lost. The neat little parlor where she had spent so many pleasant hours was dismantled

Sleeping Girl with Cat, Pierre-Auguste Renoir, 1881. French painter.

and locked up, but Juno would go, day after day, and sit on the ledge of the window-seat, looking in and mewing dolefully. She refused food; and, when too weak to mount on the sill and look in, stretched herself on the ground beneath the window, where she died for love of her mistress, as truly as any lover in an old ballad.

You see by this story the moral that I wish to convey. It is, that watchfulness, kindness, and care will develop a nature in animals such as we little dream of. Love will beget love, regular care and attention will give regular habits, and thus domestic pets may be made agreeable and interesting.

Anyone who does not feel an inclination or capacity to take the amount of care and pains necessary for the well-being of an animal ought conscientiously to abstain from having one in charge. A carefully tended pet, whether dog or cat, is a pleasant addition to the family of young people; but a neglected, ill-brought-up, ill-kept one is only an annoyance.

C H A P T E R 2

World of Wonders

No matter how much the cats fight, there always seem to be plenty of kittens.

Abraham Lincoln (1809–1865).

Even people who dislike cats find it difficult to dislike kittens. Cardinal Richelieu (1585–1642), the French statesman, liked kittens so much that he kept dozens of them for his amusement. Preferring them to cats, he replaced the kittens with more kittens as they grew older. Nor did he forget them when he died. In his will he left a large sum of money for their care and protection.

Ogden Nash, in 1940, reflected a similar preference for kittens in his poem, "The Kitten":

> The trouble with a kitten is
>
> THAT
>
> Eventually it becomes a
>
> CAT.

Although this view overlooks the many subtle virtues and the finesse of adult cats which make them so endearing, it does emphasize our perception that the difference between a kitten and a cat seems greater than the difference between other animals and their young. Whereas cats act like they know it all and tend to be rather sedate and observant, kittens are very inquisitive, energetic, and adventurous. While the disposition of the cat leans toward that of the aristocrat or philosopher, the kitten's leans more toward that of a daredevil or comedian. Because of this, kittens can be much more fun to play with—cat lovers tend to find them absolutely irresistible. All it takes is one piece of string or one paper bag; add one kitten, and the result is hours of amusement. Add another kitten and the amount of enjoyment increases logarithmically.

Kittens bring a sense of wonder to the world. Everything is new and wonderful and made just for their endless explorations. Even if they have explored something before, they will explore it again . . . and again . . . and again, each time as if it were a totally new revelation.

We were like this too when we were young. As we grow older, we lose the fresh delight in small things we had as children. We become desensitized to our surroundings. We take things for granted. And so we miss a lot of what is going on around us. Our mind learns to automatically ignore and filter out things. Kittens don't have this limitation. It takes very little to make them happy, and they never get bored with their world. They always seem to find something with which to amuse themselves.

The Kitten and Falling Leaves (excerpt)

WILLIAM WORDSWORTH, 1804. English poet.

See the Kitten on the wall,
Sporting with the leaves that fall,
Withered leaves—one—two—and three—
From the lofty elder-tree!
Through the calm and frosty air
Of this morning bright and fair,
Eddying round and round they sink
Softly, slowly: one might think,
From the motions that they made,
Every little leaf conveyed
Sylph or Faery hither tending,
To this lower world descending,
Each invisible and mute
In his wavering parachute.

Gottfried Mind (1768–1814), Swiss painter. He is called "the Raphael of Cats."

—But the Kitten, how she starts,
Crouches, stretches, paws, and darts!
First at one, and then its fellow
Just as light and just as yellow.
There are many now—now one—
Now they stop and there are none.
What intenseness of desire
In her upward eye of fire!
With a tiger-leap half-way
Now she meets the coming prey,
Lets it go as fast, and then
Has it in her power again:
Now she works with three or four,
Like an Indian conjurer;
Quick as he in feats of art,
Far beyond in joy of heart,
Were her antics played in the eye
Of a thousand standers-by,
Clapping hands with shout and stare,
What would little Tabby care
For the plaudits of the crowd!

Kittens

MICHAEL SCOT (born 1891).

Airy as leaves blown by the autumn storm,
They sprawl and frolic over the smooth grass,
Each one minutely fashioned in the form
Of feline princes of the wilderness.
The panther and the leopard and the lynx
Are imaged unmistakably in these—
The lion in the shadow of the Sphinx,
The tiger blazing forth from tropic trees.

The tendril limbs, the suave paws, soft as rain,
Recall, with every stir, similitudes
Prowling the pathless bush, the untrodden plain,
Lurking and roving in primeval woods.
The quivering stealth, the sudden pouncing springs,
The wrestling joy, the lithe grace, all betray
The ancestry of fierce untrammelled kings,
Hunting through boundless wastes, predestined prey.

The petal-ears, the eyes' quick moonstone spark,
The shell-frail jaws, the downy new-licked fur,
Each tiniest feature bears the subtle mark
Of some unvanquished forest forefather;
And, as the slight shell-echo faintly rhymes
The mighty clamour of the crashing waves,
Each purring throat diminutively mimes
The growling thunder heard in desert caves.

These are the manifest proud-blooded scions
Of beasts depicted in Assyrian rock,
The true descendants of the Hittite lions
Stone-couched in porticos of Antioch.
And moulded in no other shape than this,

Cat's World, Henriette Ronner (1821–1909). Dutch artist.

In coloured brick, great cats perambulate
Along the murals of Persepholis,
Upon the towers of the Ishtar Gate.

These silken puppets, light as puffs of smoke,
Are heirs-apparent of the fabled race
That pranced and reared in Dionysos' yoke
Across the fields of India and Thrace.
These are the wild's exiled inheritors,
Of Asian grace, of splendour African,
The breed of tameless jungle emperors,
That ruled before the dynasties of man.

Puss in Perplexity, Theophile Steinlen (1859–1923). French painter and illustrator.

A Kitten (excerpt)

AGNES REPPLIER (1855–1950). American essayist and biographer.

If "The child is father of the man," why is not the kitten father of the cat? If in the little boy there lurks the infant likeness of all that manhood will complete, why does not the kitten betray some of the attributes common to the adult puss? A puppy is but a dog, plus high spirits, and minus common sense. We never hear our friends say they love puppies, but cannot bear dogs. A kitten is a thing apart; and many people who lack the discriminating enthusiasm for cats, who regard these beautiful beasts with aversion and mistrust, are won over easily, and cajoled out of their prejudices by the deceitful wiles of kittenhood.

"The little actor cons another part," and is the most irresistible comedian in the world. Its wide-open eyes gleam with wonder and mirth. It darts madly at nothing at all, and then, as though suddenly checked in the pursuit, prances sideways on its hind legs with ridiculous agility and zeal. It makes a vast pretense of climbing the rounds of a chair and swings by the curtain like an acrobat. It scrambles up a table leg, and is seized with comic horror at finding itself full two feet from the floor. If you hasten to its rescue, it clutches you nervously, its little heart thumping against its furry sides, while its soft paws expand and contract with agitation and relief;

> And all their harmless claws disclose,
> Like prickles of an early rose.

Yet the instant it is back on the carpet it feigns to be suspicious of your interference, peers at you out of "the tail o' its ee," and scampers for protection under the sofa, from which asylum it presently emerges with cautious trailing steps, as though encompassed by fearful dangers and alarms. Its baby innocence is yet unseared. The evil knowledge of uncanny things which is the dark inheritance of cathood has not yet shadowed its round infant eyes. Where did witches find the mysterious beasts that sat motionless by their fires, and watched unblinkingly the waxen manikins dwindling in the flame? They never reared these companions of their solitude, for no witch could have endured to see a kitten gamboling on their hearthstone. A witch's kitten! That one preposterous thought proves how wide, how unfathomed, is the gap between feline infancy and age.

A Turbulent Family, Henriette Ronner (1821–1909). Dutch artist.

The Bad Kittens

ELIZABETH COATSWORTH, from *Compass Rose*, 1929. American poet.

You may call, you may call,
But the little black cats won't hear you,
The little black cats are maddened
By the bright green light of the moon,
They are whirling and running and hiding,
They are wild who were once so confiding,
They are crazed when the moon is riding—
You will not catch the kittens soon.
They care not for saucers of milk,
They think not of pillows of silk,
Your softest, crooningest call
Is less than the buzzing of flies.
They are seeing more than you see,
They are hearing more than you hear,
And out of the darkness they peer
With a goblin light in their eyes.

American cartoonist George Herriman, from *the lives and times of archy and mehitabel*, 1927. The creator of Krazy Kat. (Copyright 1934, King Features Syndicate, Inc.) Reprinted with special permission of King Features Syndicate, Inc.

On a Cat Ageing

SIR ALEXANDER GRAY, from *Gossip*, 1928. Scottish professor and poet.

He blinks upon the hearth-rug
And yawns in deep content,
Accepting all the comforts
That Providence has sent.

Louder he purrs and louder,
In one glad hymn of praise
For all the night's adventures,
For quiet, restful days.

Life will go on forever,
With all that cat can wish;
Warmth, and the glad procession
Of fish and milk and fish.

Only—the thought disturbs him—
He's noticed once or twice,
That times are somehow breeding
A nimbler race of mice.

Cat and Birds, by Harrison Weir (1824–1906). British author and Illustrator.

CHAPTER 3

Masters of Their Realm

The playful kitten, with its pretty little tigerish gambols, is infinitely more amusing than half the people one is obliged to live with in the world.

Lady Sydney Morgan (1783–1859).

If man could be crossed with the cat, it would improve man but deteriorate the cat.

Mark Twain (1835–1910).

Down through time cats have developed a very special relationship with people which is like that of no other animal. There are many animals who have been domesticated, and there are many who have refused to surrender their independence. Cats are domesticated, and yet they maintain, and seem to cherish, their aloof sovereignty.

Cats have the ability to alternate between living in the wild and living with people. Even when they live with people, they refuse to be subservient. It is said that a cat is the only domestic animal that can look a person in the eye without flinching. Perhaps this is because cats consider themselves to be our equals—or even our superiors. There is an old English proverb that says, "In the eyes of cats, all things belong to cats."

Other animals tend to fall more readily into categories: wild or domestic. It's hard, for instance, to imagine a cow living independently. A domesticated eagle seems just as odd. Cats, it seems, are determined to have the best of both worlds. This raises an interesting question: Where do people fall in this scheme? Do we live in independence, like the eagle, or has society domesticated us, like the cow? Perhaps we are a bit of both, like the cat.

Do we do as we please—eat when we're hungry and sleep when we're tired—like the cat? Could we take naps all day if we wanted to? Or do we do what's expected of us by our society—conforming our behavior to society's expectations? Whatever our answer, it may shed light on why we have such fascination for the cat and her ability to maintain the best of both worlds.

Another question comes to mind: If cats are so independent, can a person ever really own one? But maybe we're asking the wrong question. It may not be a matter of whether a cat can be owned. Instead, it may be a question of who owns whom. Do we own our cat? Or does our cat own us?

Are Cats People?

OLIVER HERFORD (1863–1935), author of *Rubaiyat of a Persian Kitten* (1904). British writer and illustrator.

If a fool be sometimes an angel unawares, may not a foolish query be a momentous question in disguise? For example, the old riddle: "Why is a hen?" which is thought by many people to be the silliest question ever asked, is in reality the most profound. It is the riddle of existence. It has an answer, to be sure, but though all the wisest men and women in the world *and* Mr. H. G. Wells have tried to guess it, the riddle "Why is a hen?" has never been answered and never will be. So, too, the question: "Are cats people?" seemingly so trivial, may be, under certain conditions, a question of vital importance.

Suppose, now, a rich man dies, leaving all his money to his eldest son, with the proviso that a certain portion of it shall be spent in the maintenance of his household as it then existed, all its members to remain under his roof, and receive the same comfort, attention or remuneration they had received in his (the testator's) lifetime. Then suppose the son, on coming into his money, and being a hater of cats, made haste to rid himself of a feline pet that had lived in the family from early kittenhood, and had been an especial favorite of his father's.

Thereupon, the second son, being a lover of cats and no hater of money, sues for possession of the estate on the ground that his brother has failed to carry out the provisions of his father's will, in refusing to maintain the household cat.

The decision of the case depends entirely on the social status of the cat.

Shall the cat be considered as a member of the household? What constitutes a household anyway?

The definition of "household" in the Standard Dictionary is as follows: *"A number of persons living under the same roof."*

If cats are people, then the cat in question is a person and a member of the household, and for failing to maintain her and provide her with the comfort and attention to which she has been used, the eldest son loses his inheritance. Having demonstrated that the question "Are cats people?" is anything but a trivial one, I now propose a court of inquiry, to settle once for all and forever, the social status of *felis domesticus*.

And I propose for the office of judge of that court—myself!

In seconding the proposal and appointing myself judge of the court, I have been careful to follow political precedent by taking no account whatever of any qualifications I may or may not have for the office.

For witnesses, I summon (from wherever they may be) two great shades, to wit: King Solomon, the wisest man of his day, and Noah Webster, the wordiest.

And I say to Mr. Webster, "Mr. Webster, what are the common terms used to designate a domestic feline whose Christian name chances to be unknown to the speaker?" and Mr. Webster answers without a moment's hesitation:

"Cat, puss, pussy and pussy-cat."

"And what is the grammatical definition of the above terms?"

"They are called nouns."

"And what, Mr. Webster, is the accepted definition of a noun?"

"A noun is the name of a person, place or thing."

"Kindly define the word 'place.' "

"A particular locality."

"And 'thing.' "

"An inanimate object."

"That will do, Mr. Webster."

So, according to Mr. Noah Webster, the entity for which the noun cat stands, must, if not a person, be a locality or an inanimate object!

A cat is surely not a locality, and as for being an inanimate object, her chance of avoiding such a condition is nine times better even than a king's.

Léopold Louis Boilly (1727–1775). French artist.

Then a cat *must* be a person.

Suppose we consult King Solomon.

In the Book of Proverbs, Chapter XXX, verse 26, Solomon says: "The coneys are but a feeble folk, yet they make their houses in the rocks."

A coney is a kind of rabbit; folk, according to Mr. Webster, only another word for people.

That settles it! If the rabbits are people, cats are people.

Long lives to the cat!

Proverb, unknown Flemish artist, 17th century.

(Untitled)

FATHER BOUGEANT (1690–1743). Jesuit priest.

. . . Such is one of those big-whiskered and well-furred tomcats, that you see quiet in a corner, digesting at his leisure, sleeping if it seems good to him, sometimes giving himself the pleasure of hunting, for the rest enjoying life peaceably, without being troubled by useless reflections, and little caring to communicate his thoughts to others. Truly it needs only that a female cat come on the scene to derange all his philosophy; but are our philosophers wiser on such occasions?

The Happy Cat

RANDALL JARRELL, 1945. American writer.

The cat's asleep; I whisper *kitten*
Till he stirs a little and begins to purr—
He doesn't wake. Today out on the limb
(The limb he thinks he can't climb down from)
He mewed until I heard him in the house.
I climbed up to get him down: he mewed.
What he says and what he sees are limited.
My own response is even more constricted.
I think, "It's lucky; what you have is too."
What do you have except—well, me?
I joke about it but it's not a joke:
The house and I are all he remembers.
Next month how will he guess that it is winter
And not just entropy, the universe
Plunging at last into its cold decline?
I cannot think of him without a pang.
That you have no more, really, than a man?
Men aren't happy: why are you?

Arthur Rackham (1867–1939),
British illustrator.

Apology for Raimond Sebonde (excerpt)

MICHEL DE MONTAIGNE, from *Essays*, 1580. French essayist.

When my cat and I entertain each other with mutual apish tricks, as playing with a garter, who knows but that I make my cat more sport than she makes me? Shall I conclude her to be simple, that has her time to begin or refuse to play as freely as I myself have? Nay, who knows but that it is a defect of my not understanding her language (for doubtless cats can talk and reason with one another) that we agree no better? And who knows but that she pities me for being no wiser than to play with her, and laughs and censures my folly for making sport for her, when we two play together?

Man with the Cat (Henry Sturgis Drinker), Cecilia Beaux, 1898.

A Letter (excerpt)

SAMUEL CLEMENS (MARK TWAIN), 1908. American writer. Twain had a number of cats, among which were Apollinaris, Beelzebub, Blatherskite, Buffalo Bill, Sour Mash, Tammany, and Zoroaster.

Redding, Connecticut,
Oct. 2, '08.

Dear Mrs. Patterson, —The contents of your letter are very pleasant and very welcome, and I thank you for them, sincerely. If I can find a photograph of my "Tammany" and her kittens, I will enclose it in this. One of them likes to be crammed into a corner-pocket of the billiard table—which he fits as snugly as does a finger in a glove and then he watches the game (and obstructs it) by the hour, and spoils many a shot by putting out his paw and changing the direction of a passing ball. Whenever a ball is in his arms, or so close to him that it cannot be played upon with risk of hurting him, the player is privileged to remove it to any one of the 3 spots that chances to be vacant. . . .

Sincerely yours,
S. L. Clemens

Mark Twain's cats, Mark Twain (1835–1910).

That Cat

BEN KING (1857–1894). American poet.

The cat that comes to my window sill
When the moon looks cold and the night is still—
He comes in a frenzied state alone
With a tail that stands like a pine tree cone,
And says: "I have finished my evening lark,
And I think I can hear a hound dog bark.
My whiskers are froze 'nd stuck to my chin.
I do wish you'd git up and let me in."
    That cat gits in.

But if in the solitude of the night
He doesn't appear to be feeling right,
And rises and stretches and seeks the floor,
And some remote corner he would explore,
And doesn't feel satisfied just because
There's no good spot for to sharpen his claws,
And meows and canters uneasy about
Beyond the least shadow of any doubt
    That cat gits out.

Siberian cats with a Russian exile.

Kitty Fisher, Nathaniel Hone, 1765.

(Untitled)

VICOMTE DE CHATEAUBRIAND in a letter to Mme. Recamier, 1829. From *Memoires d'Outres-Tombe*, 1829. When Pope Leo XII realized he was dying, he gave the French author and ambassador his cat, Micetto.

I have as companion a big greyish-red cat with black stripes across it. It was born in the Vatican, in the Raphael loggia. Leo XII brought it up in a fold of his robes where I had often looked at it enviously when the Pontiff gave me an audience. . . . It was called "the Pope's cat." In this capacity, it used to enjoy the special consideration of pious ladies. I am trying to make it forget exile, the Sistine Chapel, the sun on Michelangelo's cupola, where it used to walk, far above the earth.

(Untitled)

The COMTESSE DE CHATEAUBRIAND in a letter to M. le Moine.

You know that we have the little cat that the Pope loved so much, but which he made fast, because all they knew in the Vatican, in the way of sought-after dishes was cod and beans. . . .

Cat, Robert Leydenfrost.

The Forum on Friday

DAISY STIEBER SQUADRA, from *Cat Fancy* magazine. American poet.

At sunset, from
across the Senate steps
behind horizontal pillars
through emblazoned arches
around fragmented torsos
in the waning gold light
among breathing flowers
sprouting grass, birds, shadows—
to look at fallen kings
and lick their paws—
cats come.

Slippers, the cat with extra toes, lived in the White House during Theodore Roosevelt's administration (1901–1909).

The Cat's Dinner, Marguerite Gérard (1761–1837).

The Achievement of the Cat (excerpt)

SAKI (HECTOR HUGH MUNRO) (1870–1916), from *The Square Egg*. British humorist and satirist.

The animal which the Egyptians worshipped as divine, which the Romans venerated as a symbol of liberty, which Europeans in the ignorant Middle Ages anathematized as an agent of demonology, has displayed to all ages two closely blended characteristics—courage and self-respect. No matter how unfavorable the circumstances, both qualities are always to the fore.

Confront a child, a puppy, and a kitten with a sudden danger; the child will turn instinctively for assistance, the puppy will grovel in abject submission to the impending visitation, the kitten will brace its tiny body for a frantic resistance. And disassociate the luxury-loving cat from the atmosphere of social comfort in which it usually contrives to move, and observe it critically under the adverse conditions of civilization—that civilization which can impel a man to the degradation of clothing himself in tawdry ribald garments and capering mountebank dances in the streets for the earning of the few coins that keep him on the respectable, or non-criminal, side of society. The cat of the slums and alleys, starved, outcast, harried, still keeps amid the prowlings of its adversity the bold, free, panther-tread with which it paced of yore the temple courts of Thebes, still displays the self-reliant watchfulness which man has never taught it to lay aside.

And when its shifts and clever managings have not sufficed to stave off inexorable fate, when its enemies have proved too strong or too many for its defensive powers, it dies fighting to the last quivering with the choking rage of mastered resistance, and voicing in its death-yell that agony of bitter remonstrance which human animals, too, have flung at the powers that may be; the last protest against a destiny that might have made them happy—and has not.

Lays of Tom-Cat Hiddigeigei

JOSEPH VICTOR VON SCHEFFEL, from *Der Trompeter von Säkkingen*, 1880, translated from German.

I

When through valley and o'er mountain
Howls the storm at dead of night,
Clambering over roof and chimney,
Hiddigeigei seeks the height,
Spectre-like aloft he stands there,
Fairer than he ever seems;
From his eyes the fire-flame sparkles,
From his bristling hair it streams.

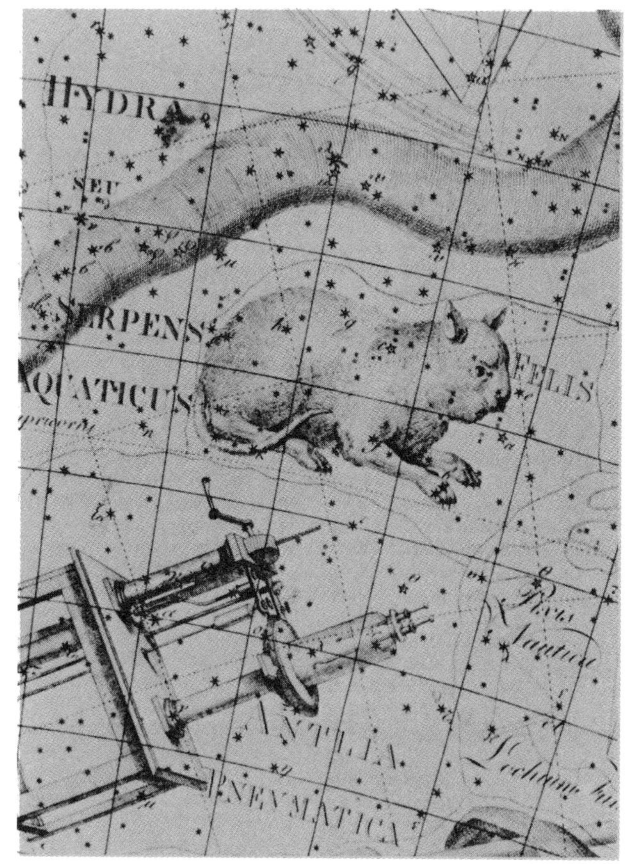

The Constellation Felis, from *Atlas Coelestis*, by J. E. Bode, 1799. French astronomer Joseph de Lalande created this constellation saying, "the large number of stars I supplied to M. Bode's charts gave me some right to shape new constellations. There were already thirty-three animals in the sky; I put in it a thirty-fourth one, the cat." Unfortunately, it never gained acceptance.

And he lifts his voice, and wildly
Sings an old cat-battle song,
That, like far-off thunder rolling,
Sweeps the storm-vexed night along.

Never a child of man can hear it—
Each sleeps heedless in his house;
But, deep down in darkest cellar,
Hears, and paling, quakes the mouse.

Well she knows the greybeard's war-cry,
Knows the cry she trembles at,
Feels how fearful in his fury
Is the grand old hero-cat.

II

From the tower's topmost angle
On the world I turn my eyes—
Mark, serene, the factions wrangle,
And the parties fall and rise.

And the keen cat's eyes they see there—
And the cat's soul feels the joke—
What dull pranks they cut beneath there,
All those petty pigmy-folk.

But what use? For I can't make 'em
See things from my point of view;
Even should the devil take 'em,
'Twill but be the devil's due.

Human nature! who can bear it?
Crooked ways and wicked wiles!
Wrapt in consciousness of merit,
Sits the tom-cat on the tiles!

CHAPTER 4

Savannas in the Suburbs

At whiles it seems as if one were somewhat as the cats, which ever have appeared to me to be animals of two parts, the one of the house and the cushion and the prepared food, the other that is free of the night and runs wild with the wind in its coat and the smell of the earth in its nostrils.

Una L. Silberrad, from *The Book of Sanchia Stapleton*, ca. 1687.

For he counteracts the Devil, who is death, by brisking about the life.
For in his morning orisons he loves the sun and the sun loves him.
For he is of the tribe of Tiger.

Christopher Smart (1722–1771), from *The Jubilate Agno* (Rejoice in the Lamb), written while he was at Bedlam, the London insane asylum.

Cats live in a twilight world between the daytime, and everyday routine of domesticity, and the dark, mysterious night of the wild. They casually slip back and forth between these two worlds. A cat who never likes to go outdoors may suddenly escape and not be seen for days. Although cats have lived with people for centuries, deep inside their cerebral cortex may lurk ancient memories of a time when their ancestors stalked the African veldts and Indonesian jungles. Today, they sit on windowsills and look out at the world, but in ways they haven't changed through the centuries. True, they now have us to feed them so they no longer have to hunt for their dinner, but they still maintain the instincts of a solitary hunter.

The role that past instincts play in the lives of cats becomes apparent when they are compared with their opposite—the dog. Dogs are social animals, running in packs rather than hunting individually. As pack animals, they are used to being part of a hierarchy and this instinct has carried over into dogs' lives with people. In their eyes, the leader of the pack has been replaced by their owner. Dogs instinctively do what their leader tells them to do. This obedience is one of the most noteworthy characteristics of dogs.

As solitary hunters, cats are loners—they only take orders from themselves. If you call them, or tell them what to do, most likely the only response you will get is an inquisitive stare, or they may ignore you altogether. Cats won't obey or learn tricks like a dog but it's not because cats are less intelligent than dogs. Intelligence has nothing to do with it—it's just that cats are their own masters. Kittens will learn tricks or games from people if they see some advantage or amusement in it. Older cats are more likely to look upon these things as utter nonsense. But a cat will learn tricks very quickly on her own if it's in her own interest. In California, I knew a cat who discovered if she rang the doorbell someone would answer and let her in. I also knew a cat in Arizona that learned to push open a latch on the backyard gate and let the dog out, probably hoping he wouldn't come back.

Cats are very territorial and tend to fight when they are kept together in close quarters. In the wild they generally live separately, getting together only to mate. Lions are the one exception to this rule. Lion prides have either one or two dominant males and may contain as many as 30 individuals. Because lions have this social heirarchy, they will learn tricks and are often the main attractions at circuses.

A major difference between lions and other pack animals is that lions expend their energy in bursts which are followed by periods of rest. They will go out hunting and briefly exert themselves capturing their prey. After eating, they often sleep for two days. Lions only need to eat about once a week and spend most of their time catnapping. Cats are also unable to sustain long periods of exertion, which is why it is difficult to take a cat out for a walk. They get tired very rapidly and you end up having to carry them most of the way. Cats are different from lions in that they eat numerous small meals throughout the day but they still follow these meals with catnaps.

Since our housecat no longer has to hunt, she may spend her hours dreaming and philosophizing. Perhaps when she sleeps, she dreams of the wild.

Indoor Jungle Blues

ULRICH TROUBETZKOY, from *The United Church Herald*, 1970.

Across the deep-piled jungle of our rooms,
he prowls the Persian patterns like a veldt
and winds his way among the window blooms
weaving the leaves and light with banded pelt.

In the striped daylight of Venetian blinds
he stalks a memory of antelope
and wildebeest, but almost never finds
a mouse to nourish atavistic hope.

Alert and cunning without need to be,
he flicks his tail, crouched on the ottoman,
ears crisped to sounds that shake tranquillity—
the pouring milk, the shearing of a can.

He prowls the tropic warmth from door to door
and stares through his transparent walls of glass
at sudden gusts of birds that dart and soar
and scatter onto fountain and the grass.

Across the indoor landscape of his days
he seeks escape from cage of pampered self,
dreams wildness, closing eyes of chrysoprase,
stretched on his high dark bough—the kitchen shelf.

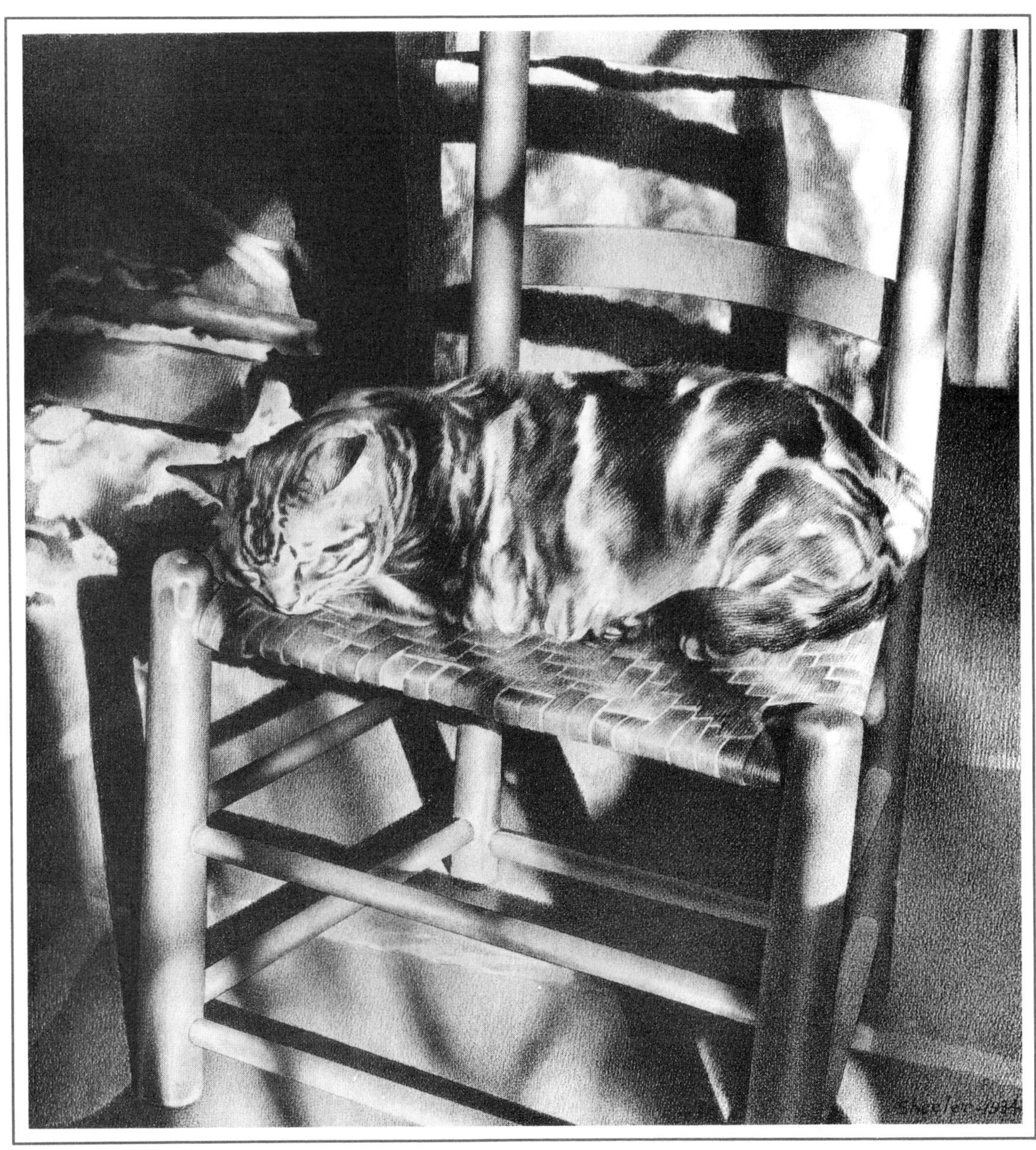

Feline Felicity, Charles Sheeler, 1934.

The Great Cats and the Bears

MAY SARTON, from *A Private Mythology*, 1966. American writer.

At night the great cats and the bears
Come out of all their secret lairs
To pad about with shining eyes
As planets bloom in darkened skies,
Their velvet paws as silent as
Footfall of moonlight on the grass,
And—shy explorers of our room—
So gently do they merge and loom
No one is startled, but each sense
Becomes electric in their presence.
All that they touch with magic paws

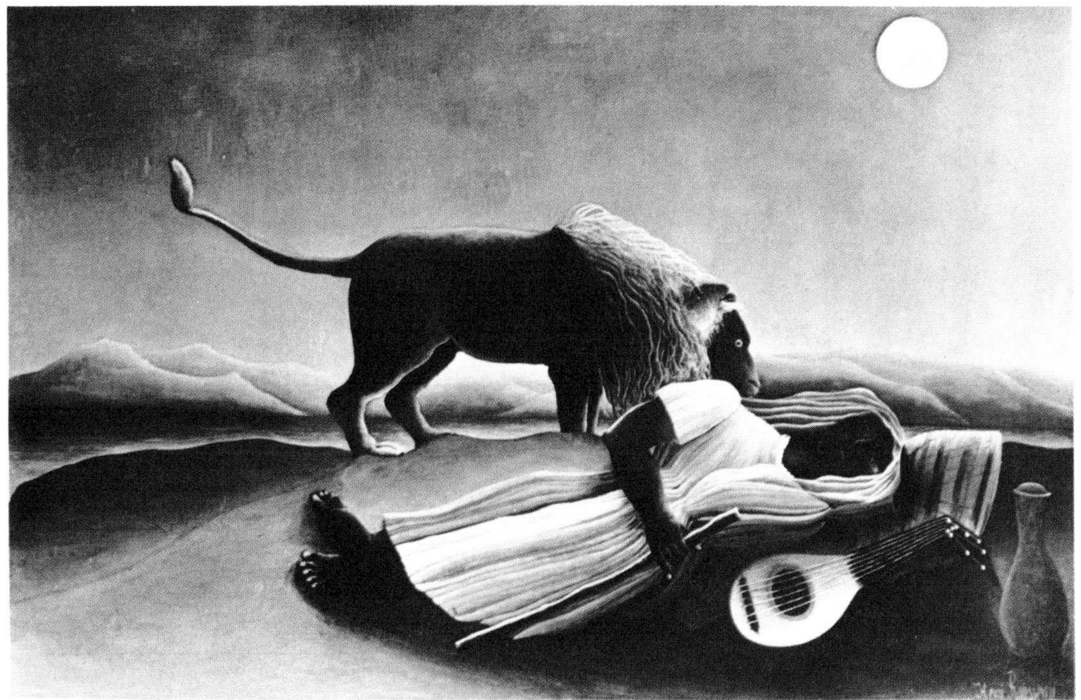

La bohémienne endormie (The Sleeping Gypsy), Henri Rousseau, 1897. French painter.

Is roused to a surprised applause,
Until upon night's inmost hour
Their fur sparks and we know their power.
The cats are roused, the bears are gay;
They take their pleasure and their play.
But what these magic ones embrace
We shall not ever know or face.
For we have fallen far below
Regions where mind can safely go.
To the primeval lairs of night
Where sense alone shines clear and bright.
And in the faint light of the dawn,
The great cats and the bears are gone.

Edward Gorey, from *Old Possum's Book of Practical Cats*, 1982.

The Cat That Walked by Himself (excerpt)

RUDYARD KIPLING, from *Just So Stories*, 1902. English author.

He will kill Mice and he will be kind to Babies when he is in the house, as long as they do not pull his tail too hard. But when he has done that, and between times, he is the Cat that walks by himself and all places are alike to him, and if you look out at nights you can see him waving his wild tail and walking by his wild lone—just the same as before.

The Greater Cats

VICTORIA SACKVILLE-WEST (1892–1962). English novelist and poet.

The greater cats with golden eyes
Stare out between the bars.
Deserts are there, and different skies,
And night with different stars.
They prowl the aromatic hill,
And mate as fiercely as they kill,
And hold the freedom of their will
To roam, to live, to drink their fill;
But this beyond their wit know I:
Man loves a little, and for long shall die.

A Bacchante, Arthur Wardle, ca. 1907.

Their kind across the desert range
Where tulips spring from stones,
Not knowing they will suffer change
Or vultures pick their bones.
Their strength's eternal in their sight
They rule the terror of the night,
They overtake the deer in flight,
And in their arrogance they smite;
But I am sage, if they are strong;
Man's love is transient as his death is long.

Yet oh, what powers to deceive!
My wit is turned to faith,
And at this moment I believe
In love, and scout at death.
I came from nowhere, and shall be
Strong, steadfast, swift, eternally:
I am a lion, a stone, a tree,
And as the Polar star in me
Is fixed my constant heart on thee.
Ah, may I stay for ever blind
With lions, tiger, leopards, and their kind.

The Black Panther

(from Leconte de Lisle)

RICHMOND LATTIMORE, from *Poems from Three Decades*, 1951. American poet.

Pallors of rose widen across the sky
along its eastern margin crinkles with fresh light,
and, in a shower of drops resolved, merge in the sea
    pearls from the necklace of the night.

Now all one quarter of the sky, sheathed in soft flames,
gathers to gold on the blue glitter of its spire.
One lingering fold, ablush against the green of gems,
    whelms all in dripping rain of fire.

And from the bamboos that wake against the beating wings
of wind, and lichees purple-fruited, and upon
cinnamon trees where dews are bunched in glittering
    globes, swarm the fresh murmurs of the dawn.

From wood and hillside, flowers, from height of moss along
the soft and subtle atmosphere, begins a flight,
from air suddenly troubled, of odors sweet and strong,
    fevered with promise of delight.

There, where all paths are lost in virgin growth of trees
and thick grass streams against the sun in morning glades,
by streams quick-running deep between declivities,
    beneath rattans in green arcades,

she goes, the queen of Java, the dark huntress. Dawn
sees her return to the lair, where her little ones
disconsolately yowl heap-huddled, one upon
    another, nested in shining bones.

Edmond Dulac, from *The Story of the Stone Prince*, ca. 1907.

Watchful, with eyes barbed like arrows, in sinuous stride
she walks among the glooms of heavy boughs, restless,
with fresh blood spattered here and there along her side
and damp upon her velvet dress.

She drags with her a remnant of the beast she killed
and fed on in the night, quarter and half the back
of a grand stag. On moss and flower, grim traces spilled,
red, wet, and warm still, stain her track.

Above, brown bees and butterflies, in rivalry
of play, flutter against and brush with wings the flow
of her back. Fronds in a thousand corbeils joyously
    perfume the ground where her pads go.

And, mail uncoiling from the middle of his red
thicket of thorns, to watch above surrounding grasses,
the python rears a flat and interested head,
    but keeps his distance as she passes.

Under the towering fern she slithers out of sight
without noise. The mossed stalks bend as she shoulders by.
Sounds fall silent; the air burns; the enormous light
    sleeps on the forest and the sky.

Wildcat

FRANCES COLVIN, from *Yankee* magazine, 1965. American poet.

A wildcat lurks behind this hillside town;
His golden eyes are flowers in the dark
And stripes run from the trees into his fur,
Furrowed like piney-bark in black and brown.
How big he is, no one can rightly say—
But big enough to frighten and delight;
And like a wild rose vine his thorny track
Is found long after he has gone away.
His boundaries are altered by his will;
The town seems wider while the cat's at large
Within a necessary wilderness
And we remember there remains a hill
No man has walked on yet. We let him range
The province of our willful ignorance,
Above geraniumed streets, out of our sight,
Dark disarranger of our dreams at night.

Roman statue of a cat and a snake, 100 B.C. to A.D. 200.

The Cat

PHILIP DACEY, from *Cat Fancy* magazine, 1971. American poet and professor.

He has a history
of long, silent
descending
from trees.
He lands

years later
in the laps of women.
He brings with him
a memory
of waiting deep in leaves,

of bright claws he now
is amazed to find
grown short and tucked
like pale fingers
into the folds of a dress

He has fallen
out of life.
He tries to remember
a lake in a clearing,
but each time he would drink

from that memory he discovers
in a blue saucer of milk
his face like a head
served up on a plate.

Henriette Ronner (1821–1909), Dutch artist.

Studies of a Cat, Thomas Gainsborough, 1760s. British painter.

Charcoal Sketch

MICHAEL SCOT (born 1891).

Uplifting suddenly slim fiery-golden anthers,
Scarlet hibiscus-buds of Indian dawn unfolded,
And in their deep-blue-shadowed jungle lair, dark panthers
Unlidded waking eyes, more fiercely fiery-golden.

The hidden stormwind of their tautened muscles moved
Under the thundercloud of drowsy velvet fur,
Carving sleek lissom flanks with hungry ribs and grooves,
Chiseling silken limbs to frolic hunting curves.

Sleepily flaring open yawning sable jaws,
They gaped abysmal caves, flaming geranium,
And tossing slumber-dusk from sun-glossed lazy paws,
Outsprayed the sabre claws, ablaze with mirrored sun.

* * *

Their sun-awakened splendour dazzled in the room
Just for a timeless instant when the firelight broke,
Suddenly smouldering, from midnight charcoal gloom,
Blossoming glowingly through grey enclouding smoke,

Unfolding delicately, scarlet ember buds,
Lifting thin anther-flames of mimic Eastern dawn,
Waking the young black cat upon the sapphire rug
To open fiery-golden eyes, and, stretching, yawn.

C H A P T E R 5

Lurking in the Shadows

The Mouse should stand in Feare,
So should the squeaking Rat;
All this would I doe if I were
Converted to a Cat.

George Turberville (ca. 1540–1610), from *The Lover, Whose Mistresse Feared a Mouse, Declareth That He Would Become a Cat if He Might Have His Desire.*

How do you spell mousetrap in three letters?

An old riddle.

The Egyptians first became interested in cats probably because of the cat's ability to solve mouse and rat problems. Later, the Egyptians came to appreciate cats for other reasons and even worshipped them as gods. In Europe at this time, weasels and skunks were the only pest controllers. Although the Europeans continually tried to talk the Egyptians out of a few cats, they were unsuccessful because the Egyptians had a law making it illegal to export a cat. In fact, the Egyptians sent soldiers abroad to capture all the cats they could get their hands on. Eventually, around 1500 B.C., the Greeks stole about a dozen cats and soon began to trade them with the Romans, Gauls, and Celts. The Romans captured some during their invasions of Egypt and carried them home as pampered pets, where they became the Roman symbol for liberty. By the 1st century A.D. cats had become popular in Rome, although Julius Caesar (100–44 B.C.) was said to have been afraid of them.

Cats soon spread throughout the known world. The Phoenicians were the first to take cats to the British Isles, where they were traded for tin from Cornish mines. Around A.D. 300 the Romans also brought them to Britain. They reached China in about A.D. 400 and became a symbol of peace, fortune, and family serenity. The Japanese used cats in temples to guard their sacred manuscripts.

From the time cats were first introduced in Japan, around A.D. 999, until the 17th century, they were always kept on silk leashes. They were considered too valuable to be allowed to run loose. It took a royal decree to release them. Rats and mice had all but destroyed the silk industry, seriously damaging the granaries and food stores. Japan's economy was on the brink of collapse. The Japanese government ordered all cats to be released; anyone caught buying or selling a cat had to pay a fine. Once free, the cats soon had the rats and mice under control.

In Europe the cat began to be persecuted by the Roman Catholic church. Even though Saint Patrick (ca. 389–461) and Pope Gregory the Great (ca. 540–604) had been avid cat lovers, the church began to associate cats with Satan. Live cats were thrown on bonfires at holidays and festivals. By the mid-13th century, the Nordic cult of Freyja, a fertility goddess, was being revived in the Rhineland. The worshippers of Freyja, along with the Knights Templars (Masons), were accused of cat worship and were actively persecuted by the Inquisition.

Cats later became a general symbol of heresy. In the time of Queen Mary I (Bloody Mary, 1516–1558), cats were burned as a symbol of Protestant heresy. Queen Elizabeth I (1533–1603) had a wicker effigy of the pope, filled with live cats, burned at her coronation as a symbol of Catholic heresy. The witch trials also raged out of control at this time.

By 1400 the cat was perilously close to extinction—but she was saved by the plague. Crusaders returning from the Holy Wars had brought back black rats aboard their ships. With the shortage of cats, the rats spread rapidly. The Black Death struck Europe from 1346 to 1349 and wiped out about 25 million people, almost half of Europe. Plagues continued to sweep across Europe until the Great Plague of 1665, which killed half of London. Although cats continued to be burned, they were tolerated as the only answer to the plagues. In the end it was the cat's ability to control pests that saved them from extinction.

Loving and Liking (excerpt)

WILLIAM WORDSWORTH, 1832. British poet.

Long may you love your pensioner mouse,
Though one of a tribe that torment the house:
Nor dislike for her cruel sport the cat,
Deadly foe both of mouse and rat;
Remember she follows the law of her kind,
And Instinct is neither wayward nor blind.
Then think of her beautiful gliding form,
Her tread that would scarcely crush a worm,
And her soothing song by the winter fire,
Soft as the dying throb of the lyre.

Cat Stalking Mouse, Henri de Toulouse-Lautrec (1864–1901). French painter.

16th-century woodcut.

. . . And the Mouse Police Never Sleeps

IAN ANDERSON, from *Heavy Horses*, 1978. British musician (of Jethro Tull).

Muscled, black with steel-green eye
Swishing through the rye grass
    with thoughts of mouse-and-apple pie
Tail balancing at half-mast.
. . . And the mouse police never sleeps
    lying in the cherry tree.

Savage bed foot-warmer
    of purest feline ancestry.
Look out, little furry folk!
He's the all-night working cat
Eats but one in every ten
    leaves the others on the mat.

. . . And the mouse police never sleeps
    waiting by the cellar door.
Window-box town-crier;
    birth and death registrar.
With claws that rake a furrow red
Licensed to mutilate.
From warm milk on a lazy day
    to dawn patrol on hungry hate
. . . No, the mouse police never sleeps
    climbing on the ivy.
Windy roof-top weathercock
Warm-blooded night on a cold tile.

The Cat with the Wooden Paw

WENDELL MARGRAVE of Carbondale, Illinois, 1938.

Jack Storme was the local cooper and blacksmith of Thebes. He had a cat that stayed around the shop. The cat was the best mouser in the whole country, Jack said. He kept the shop free of rats and mice. But one day the cat got a forepaw cut off. After that he began to grow poor and thin and didn't take any interest in anything because he wasn't getting enough to eat.

So one day Jack decided to fix him up a wooden paw. He whittled one out with his knife and strapped it on the maimed leg. After that the cat began to grow sleek and fat again. Jack decided to stay at the shop one night to see how the cat managed it with his wooden paw.

After dark the cat got down in front of a mouse-hole and waited. Pretty soon a mouse peered out cautiously. Quick as a flash the cat seized it with his good paw and knocked it on the head with his wooden one. In no time that cat had eighteen mice piled up before the hole.

Drawing by Chas. Addams. © 1975 *The New Yorker Magazine, Inc.*

Henriette Ronner (1821–1909), Dutch artist.

Man Meets Dog (excerpt)

KONRAD LORENZ, 1954. Austrian behaviorist.

Thus the short feline attack is only to gain time while finding a way of escape. There is, however, one contingency in which a cat may make a prolonged and earnest attack in this hunchbacked attitude, and that is when she is defending her young. In this case she approaches her enemy when he is some distance away and she moves in a peculiar fashion, galloping with an up and down and sideways motion, for she must continually present her imposing broadside to the foe. Though this broadside gallop with laterally held tail is seldom to be seen in real earnest, it can very often be observed in the play of young cats. I have never seen it in mature tomcats except in play, for there is no situation in which they are obliged to attack an enemy like this. In the suckling female cat, this broadside attack brings with it an absolute and unconditional readiness for self-sacrifice, and, in this state, even the gentlest cat is almost invincible. I have seen large dogs, notorious cat killers, capitulate and flee before such an attack. Ernest Thompson Seton graphically describes a charming and doubtless true occurrence in which a mother cat in Yellowstone Park put a bear to flight and pursued him until he climbed a tree in terror.

Ailurophiles, Ailurophobes (excerpt)

ROGER A. CARAS, from *A Celebration of Cats*, 1986. Author and television news correspondent.

Tradition has it that Adolf Hitler hated cats. He probably did; everything else was wrong with him. Napoleon also hated cats. There are endlessly repeated stories about the French emperor and his problem. On one such occasion, it is said, he was heard calling hoarsely for help from his tent. Aides rushed in expecting to find an assassin at work and found Napoleon alone instead, sword drawn, doing battle with the rich tapestry hangings he enjoyed having around him. He insisted he had either seen or could sense a cat lurking somewhere behind them. He was gasping for breath, red in the face, near collapse. He had to be helped to his bed, and a doctor was called in to settle him down. How much of that is just more Napoleonic lore, of which there is a great deal, and how much truth is difficult to determine, but clearly the man who would conquer the world could not overcome an unreasoning dread of a small, harmless companion animal.

It is interesting that Napoleon and Hitler shared this fear, because a third would-be conqueror of the world, Alexander the Great, is supposed to have been numbered among the world's premier ailurophobes as well. It is said that he would swoon at the sight of a cat. Fearless before armies, indifferent to personal danger, the man who legend says wept because there were no more nations to conquer, no more armies to annihilate, was terrified of a house cat.

What is there about the cat that so threatens, or perhaps frustrates, world conquerors?

Peruvian painting on a cloak, ca. A.D. 100.

CHAPTER 6

Legends Through the Hourglass

If a cat cross his path he will not proceed on his way.

Theoprastus, 319 B.C.

Cats have long been the subject of superstitions and myths. Many of the beliefs and stories stemmed from the association of cats with witchcraft and from cats' having been persecuted and burned in the Middle Ages. Other ideas no doubt sprang from the universal human need to explain anything that is mysterious, such as the behavior of a cat.

In the United States black cats were thought to be unlucky, especially if they crossed your path, whereas in England white cats were unlucky. In Northern Europe it was unlucky if a cat crossed your path from the left but lucky if the cat came from the right. In Canada cats of three colors were lucky, whereas tortoiseshell cats were lucky for the Japanese. In Northern Europe it was a good sign if a strange cat entered a house on its own volition. Calicos were considered lucky for sailors. In China the older and uglier a cat, the luckier. To the Buddhists all cats were lucky; the dark ones were thought to bring gold, the light ones to bring silver.

In the lore of Abyssinia, any unmarried girl who owned a cat was a wealthy catch for bachelors. In Britain the "blackberry" cat, born at the end of the blackberry season, was said to be notorious for getting into mischief. According to an old legend, it was this time of year that Satan was tossed out of heaven and landed on earth in a blackberry bush. Any kitten born in May was thought to be a poor hunter who would bring home glowworms or snakes instead of mice. May kittens were usually drowned.

In the southern United States if you kicked a cat you would get rheumatism, and if you drowned a cat the Devil would get you. It was also believed that on the tip of a cat's tail were three hairs of the Devil, which caused cats to prowl at night. In the northern United States cat's eyes were used to tell the tides. If the pupils were contracted it was high tide, if dilated the tide was ebbing.

Cats were also used to predict the weather. If a cat washed behind her ears, if she winked, or if she sneezed once, there would be rain. If she ran about in a wild manner, it would be windy. If she sat with her back to the fire, there would be frost or storms. Sailors thought if a black cat fell overboard it would cause a storm, and Indonesians believed they could cause rain by pouring water on a cat.

A Slavic myth had it that cats became possessed by demons during a thunderstorm. The thunder carried the prayers of the angels, which were mocked by the possessed cats; so the angels aimed lightning bolts at the cats to cast out the demons. During storms the people would chase cats away from their houses to prevent their homes from being hit by the lightning.

People have always used myths and legends to explain things they didn't understand—and the peculiarities of cats are no exception. A Jewish myth tells how cats were sneezed forth by the lions on Noah's ark and therefore were not created by God, which explains their strange behavior. Fables, such as those of Aesop and Pilpay, were used as instruction and advice, and, once again, cats played a role.

The Cat-Maiden

AESOP (ca. 619–564 B.C.), from *Aesop's Fables*. Greek fabulist.

The gods were once disputing whether it was possible for a living being to change its nature. Jupiter said "Yes," but Venus said "No." So, to try the question, Jupiter turned a Cat into a Maiden, and gave her to a young man for a wife. The wedding was duly performed and the young couple sat down to the wedding-feast. "See," said Jupiter to Venus, "how becomingly she behaves. Who could tell that yesterday she was but a Cat? Surely her nature is changed?"

"Wait a minute," replied Venus, and let loose a mouse into the room. No sooner did the bride see this than she jumped up from her seat and tried to pounce upon the mouse. "Ah, you see," said Venus, "Nothing can change one's real nature."

Roman mosaic from Pompeii, ca. 100 B.C.

The Greedy and Ambitious Cat

PILPAY, *Fable III*, ca. 300 B.C. Oriental fabulist.

There was formerly an old woman in a village, extremely thin, half-starved, and meager. She lived in a little cottage as dark and gloomy as a fool's heart, and withal as close shut up as a miser's hand. This miserable creature had for the companion of her wretched retirements a cat meager and lean as herself; the poor creature never saw bread nor beheld the face of a stranger, and was forced to be contented with only smelling the mice in their holes, or seeing the prints of their feet in the dust. If by some extraordinary lucky chance this miserable animal happened to catch a mouse, she was like a beggar that discovers a treasure; her visage and her eyes were inflamed with joy, and that booty served her for a whole week; and out of the excess of her admiration, and distrust of her own happiness, she would cry out to herself, "Heavens! Is this a dream, or is it real?" One day, however, ready to die for hunger, she got upon the ridge of her enchanted castle, which had long been the mansion of famine for cats, and spied from thence another cat, that was stalking upon a neighbor's wall like a lion, walking along as if she had been counting her steps, and so fat that she could hardly go. The old woman's cat, astonished to see a creature of her own species so plump and large, with a loud voice, cried out to her pussy neighbor, "In the name of pity, speak to me, thou happiest of the cat kind! Why, you look as if you came from one of the Khan of Kathai's feasts; I conjure ye, to tell me how, or in what region it is that you get your skin so well stuffed?" "Where?" replied the fat one; "Why, where should one feed well but at a king's table? I go to the house," continued she, "every day about dinner-time, and there I lay my paws upon some delicious morsel or other, which serves me till the next, and then leave enough for an army of mice, which under me live in peace and tranquility; for why should I commit murder for a piece of tough and skinny mouse flesh, when I can live on venison at a much easier rate?" The lean

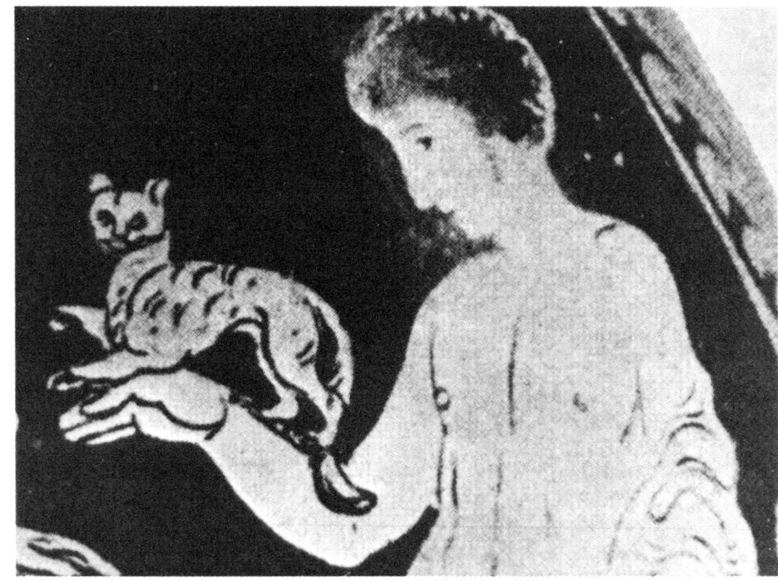

Detail from a Grecian plate.

cat, on this, eagerly inquired the way to this house of plenty, and entreated her plump neighbor to carry her one day along with her. "Most willingly," said the fat puss; "for thou seest I am naturally charitable, and thou art so lean that I heartily pity thy condition." On this promise they parted and the lean cat returned to the old woman's chamber, where she told her dame the story of what had befallen her. The old woman prudently endeavored to persuade her cat from prosecuting her design, admonishing her withal to have a care of being deceived; "For, believe me," said she, "the desires of the ambitious are never to be satiated, but when their mouths are stuffed with the dirt of their graves. Sobriety and temperance are the only things that truly enrich people. I must tell thee, poor silly cat, that they who travel to satisfy their ambition have no knowledge of the good things they possess, nor are they truly thankful to heaven for what they enjoy, who are not contented with their fortune."

The poor starved cat, however, had conceived so fair an idea of the king's table, that the old woman's good morals and judicious remonstrances entered in at one ear and went out at the other. In short, she departed the next day with the fat puss to go to the king's house; but, alas! before she got thither, her destiny had laid a snare for her. For being a house of good cheer, it was so haunted with cats that the servants had, just at this time orders to kill all the cats that came near it, by reason of a great robbery committed the night before in the king's larder by several grimalkins. The old woman's cat, however, pushed on by hunger, entered the house, and no sooner saw a dish of meat unobserved by the cooks, but she made a seizure of it, and was doing what for many years she had not done before, that is, heartily filling her belly; but as she was enjoying herself under the dresser-board, and feeding heartily upon her stolen morsels, one of the testy officers of the kitchen, missing his breakfast, and seeing where the poor cat was solacing herself with it, threw his knife at her with such an unlucky hand, that he struck her full in the breast. However, as it has been the providence of nature to give this creature nine lives instead of one, poor puss made a shift to crawl away, after she had for some time shammed dead: but, in her flight, observing the blood come streaming from her wound: "Well," said she, "let me but escape this accident, and if ever I quit my old hold and my own mice for all the rarities in the king's kitchen, may I lose all of my nine lives at once."

The Splinter Cat (*Felynx arbordiffisus*)

WILLIAM T. COX, from *Fearsome Creatures of the Lumberwoods, with a Few Desert and Mountain Beasts*, 1910. American writer.

A widely distributed and frightfully destructive animal is the splinter cat. It is found from the Great Lakes to the Gulf, and eastward to the Atlantic Ocean, but in the Rocky Mountains has been reported from only a few localities. Apparently the splinter cat inhabits that part of the country in which wild bees and raccoons abound. These are its natural food, and the animal puts in every dark and stormy night shattering trees in search of coons or honey. It doesn't use any judgment in selecting coon trees or bee trees, but just smashes one tree after another until a hollow one containing food is found. The method used by this animal in its destructive work is simple but effective. It climbs one tree, and from the uppermost branches bounds down and across toward the tree it wishes to destroy. Striking squarely with its hard face, the splinter cat passes right on, leaving the tree broken and shattered as though struck by lightning or snapped off by the wind. Appalling destruction has been wrought by this animal in the Gulf States, where its work in the shape of a wrecked forest is often ascribed to windstorms.

Arthur Rackham, from *Irish Fairy Tales*, 1920. British illustrator.

The Cactus Cat (*Cactifelinus inebrius*)

WILLIAM T. COX

How many people have heard of the cactus cat? Thousands of people spend their winters in the great Southwest—the land of desert and mountain, of fruitful valleys, of flat-topped mesas, of Pueblos, Navajos, and Apaches, of sunshine, and the ruins of ancient "Cliff-dwellers." It is doubtful, however, if one in a hundred of these people ever heard of a cactus cat, to say nothing of seeing one sporting about among the cholla and palo verde. Only the old-timers know of the beast and its queer habits.

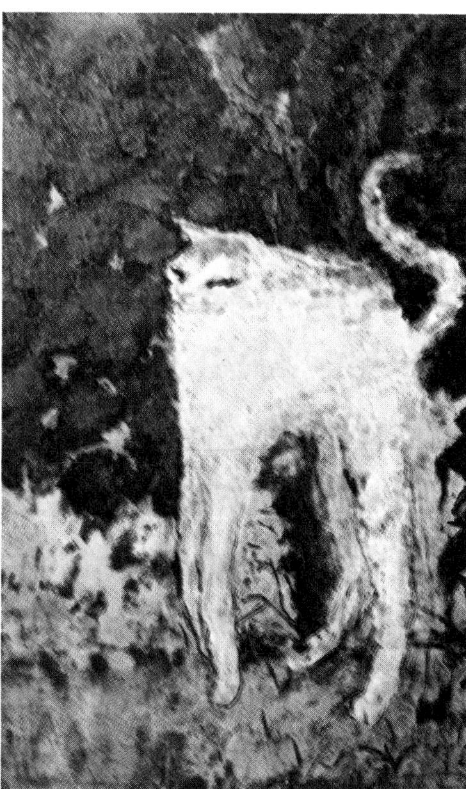

The Cat, Pierre Bonnard, 1894. French artist.

The cactus cat, as its name signifies, lives in the great cactus districts, and is particularly abundant between Prescott and Tucson. It has been reported, also, from the valley of the lower Yaqui, in Old Mexico, and the cholla-covered hills of Yucatán. The cactus cat has thorny hair, the thorns being especially long and rigid on its ears. Its tail is branched and upon the forearms above its front feet are sharp, knifelike blades of bone. With these blades it slashes the base of giant cactus trees, causing the sap to exude. This is done systematically, many trees being slashed in the course of several nights as the cat makes a big circuit. By the time it is back to the place of beginning, the sap of the first cactus has fermented into a kind of mescal, sweet and very intoxicating. This is greedily lapped up by the thirsty beast, which soon becomes fiddling drunk, and goes waltzing off in the moonlight, rasping its bony forearms across each other and screaming with delight.

Hopi Folk Tale

Onyx statue, from Teotihuacan, Mexico, 100 B.C. to A.D. 750.

A long time ago a Hopi boy went out to hunt. It was winter, and snow lay on the ground in the valley where he searched for game. To his surprise he found some tracks in it that were like no tracks he had ever seen before, and he followed them. Out of the valley they went, ending at last at a large rock. The boy put his hand into the opening under the rock and pulled out a strange animal by its leg. He tied its legs together and started back with it to his village.

When he reached home and asked his father what the animal was he was told that it was a cat and that it ate mice, rats and rabbits. On hearing this the boy went again into the valley and caught a rabbit which he brought back to the cat.

Keeping it confined in a niche in the wall of his home he continued to feed it for four days. In this way the cat became tame and has lived in Hopi houses ever since.

The Four-Eyed Cat

An old British legend as told in 1955 by N. Marchant (age 12), daughter of a lightship sailor from Essex County, who learned it from her grandparents. It is a general belief of fishermen all round the British Isles that it is unlucky to take a woman to the fishing grounds or to meet one on the way to sea. In some places the taboo extends even to mentioning a woman.

There was a gentleman had a beautiful daughter who was bad at heart, and they said she knew more than a Christian should, and they wanted to swim her [*a test where a suspected witch was cast into water—if she sank she was innocent, if she floated she was a witch*], but no one dared because of her father. She drew a spell on a poor fisherman, and he followed for love of her wherever she went. He deserted his troth-plight maid, though he was to be married in a week, and he ran away to sea with the gentleman's daughter and unbeknown to all the rest (that is, the rest of the fleet) took her out with them to the fishing. She did it to spite her father's pride, but he thought himself well rid of her.

A storm blew up and the whole fishing fleet were lost to a man for they had on board a woman with them at sea, though none knew of it but her lover. It was she that had whistled up the storm that had drowned her own lover, for she hated everyone. She was turned into a four-eyed cat, and ever after she haunted the fishing fleet.

So that is why even now fishermen won't cast their nets before half-past three (cock-crow)—my uncles won't—and they always throw a bit back into the sea for the cat.

Cat Fight in a Larder, Paulos de Vos.

CHAPTER 7

Castles and Princesses

The cat's winged yearnings journey,
Unrestrained o'er Time and Space.

Hiddigeigei, a Tom-cat in *Der Trompeter von Säkkingen*, by Joseph Victor von Scheffel, 1880.

You got the wrong cat by the tail that time.

Kathleen Knight, *Rendezvous with the Past*, 1940.

Cats have appeared in fairy tales through the years, usually in small, incidental roles. In a few tales the cat has played a central character, the most famous being *Puss in Boots* and *Dick Whittington and His Cat*. Cats appear in a variation of the Cinderella story, where a young girl with an abusive mother and a mean sister is required to take care of a castle full of cats. She is rewarded for her hard work with gifts of gold and jewels, which she gives to her family. Her sister goes to the castle hoping for the same reward, but her laziness and abuse of the cats only earn her a dunking in oil and permanent ugliness. The young girl returns to take care of the cats and lives happily ever after.

In another tale King Arthur slaughters the Demon Cat of Losanne, France. In the French version of this tale, the story ends with the cat defeating King Arthur and carrying him away. A story from Siam attributes the shadowy patches on the necks of Siamese cats to thumbprints left by the gods when they picked up the cats to admire them.

A wonderful Chinese tale tells of a time when cats were the rulers of the world. Back then, cats had the ability to speak and people couldn't. The cats handled all of the everyday affairs of the planet, but they soon decided they would much rather bask in the sun to warm themselves and take catnaps than have to worry about governing the earth. So they looked all around and decided to leave the care of the world to humans. In order for humankind to be able to take over the job, the cats gave people the ability to talk, which they in turn lost. Now people take care of the earth, and cats spend their time doing what they enjoy most. Some say this is why they always seem to be smiling at us.

Cats were considered to have a strong connection with the world of fairies. In Ireland some people believed that cats were fairies, and in Scotland stories were told of goblins who had the form of cats. The Celts believed the cat's tail was extremely potent and that if you accidentally stepped on it, a serpent would rise up and strike you dead.

On the Isle of Man it's said that the fairies, who generally dislike having people around, accept cats because cats can see ghosts and wraiths after dark. Because of this acceptance, the fairies allow cats to stay with them when they come into people's kitchens at night. In fact, if a family puts the cat out before they go to bed, the fairies will often let it back in again.

The Celts believed that the eyes of a cat acted like telepathic windows to the palaces of fairy kings. These kings could look out and watch our world through the cat's eyes and could keep track of what people were doing. This belief also explained why cats tended to watch people so closely. These cat-eye windows worked both ways. If you looked deeply into a cat's eyes, you could see the strangely illuminated world of the fairies.

Gagliuso: A Fairy Tale from the Pentameron

The story of *Puss in Boots*, which originally came from India, appeared in four major versions from the early 16th century to the middle of the 18th century. The most famous version was written by Charles Perrault in the 1590s. *Gagliuso* is a version written in the early 1500s by Giambattista Basile. It contains an ending that is substantially different from Perrault's version.

There once lived in Naples a poor old man named Gagliuso, so squalid and destitute that he was as naked as a worm. Feeling himself at the point of death, he said to his two children, Oratiello and Pippo, "My sons, I am summoned to pay the debt of nature. Believe me, Christians as you are, that my only regret in quitting this sad abode of toil and pain is that I leave you without a farthing. Alas! you will have less than a fly could carry off on his foot. I have led a dog's life; I have dined off an empty stomach, and gone to bed in the dark. But in spite of all, I wish on my deathbed to leave you some token of my love. Oratiello, my firstborn, take that wallet hanging on the wall, and may you find in it every night what I have often sought in vain all day, a crust of bread. As to you, my youngest, take the cat. My children, remember your dear father." With these words, he burst into tears, and a little while after said, "Farewell, it is night."

Oratiello buried his father at the public expense; after which he plucked up his courage, and went down to the bay to help the fishermen draw the seine.

But Pippo, looking at the cat, cried, "See what a fine legacy my father has left me! I cannot keep myself, and here I have two mouths to feed!"

The cat heard these lamentations, and remarked, "You complain without cause, and have more luck than sense. You do not know your good-fortune, for I can make you rich if I set about it."

Pippo felt that she was right. He stroked the cat three or four times, and warmly besought the favor of Dame Puss, who took

German engraving from *Puss in Boots*.

compassion on the poor lad. She went out every morning, to the bay, or the fish-market, where she managed to lay hold of some large mullet or superb sword-fish, which she carried to the king, saying, "Your majesty's slave, Signor Gagliuso, sends this fish, with his compliments, as a small gift to a great prince."

Upon which the king, with the pleased air of one receiving a present, would answer, "Tell this stranger gentleman that I am infinitely obliged to him."

Another time the cat would scour the fields and marshes, and when the hunters shot down a blackbird, lark, or woodcock, would snatch up the game, and hurry with it on the same errand to the king. She used this artifice so long that at last, one morning, the king said, "I am under so many obligations to Signor Gagliuso, that I should like to make his acquaintance and thank him for all his courtesy." The cat replied, "Signor Gagliuso's blood and life are at your majesty's disposal. My master will wait upon you tomorrow morning without fail."

Morning having come, the cat hastened to the king, crying, "Signor Gagliuso begs you to excuse him for not presenting himself before you. Some of his rascally valets ran off with his clothes last night; the thieves have not left him a shirt to his back."

On hearing this, the king ordered a quantity of linen and wearing apparel to be taken from his own wardrobe and sent to Gagliuso. Before two hours had passed our hero entered the palace, escorted by the cat. The king received him most graciously, and seating him by his side, ordered a magnificent feast to be served him.

While they were at dinner, Gagliuso turned from time to time to the cat, and said, "Look here, Puss, keep an eye on our things!" to which she answered, "Hush! hush! don't speak of such trifles." The king asked what troubled Gagliuso, whereupon the cat said that he would like a small lemon, when the king sent to the garden for a whole basketful. But Gagliuso continued to repeat the same thing, while the cat tried to hush him, and when the king insisted upon knowing what was the matter, invented one excuse after another to conceal her master's meanness, in thinking that anyone there would be likely to steal his hat and cloak.

At last, after sitting long at the table, talking of one thing and another, Gagliuso asked permission to withdraw. Left alone with the king, the cat extolled her master's merit, wit, and good sense, and above all, the immense wealth that he possessed in the Roman Campagna and Lombardy. He was just such a son-in-law as a crowned head might desire. The king, asking what his fortune

Li Ti, A.D. 1174. Chinese artist.

might be, the cat declared that it was impossible to reckon the value of the goods and chattels of this Croesus, who did not know himself what he was worth. But if the king wished to be sure, it was a very easy matter; he had only to send some trusty messengers across the frontier, and they would learn for themselves that there was no wealth in the world like Gagliuso's.

The king summoned his faithful counsellors, and ordered them carefully to inquire into the affair. They followed the cat, who, as soon as they had crossed the frontier, ran on before, on the pretense of preparing refreshments. Wherever she found a flock of sheep, cows, horses, or swine, she said to the shepherds, or keepers, "Look here! there is a company of robbers coming to plunder everything they find. If you wish to escape and save your property, you must say, 'All this belongs to Signor Gagliuso!' and they will not touch a hair."

She repeated the same thing at all the farms along the way, so that, wherever the king's messengers went, they heard the same song. All that they saw belonged to Signor Gagliuso. Tired of asking the same question, they returned to the king and told him wonders concerning Signor Gagliuso's possessions. On hearing this the monarch promised the cat a heavy fee if she would make the match, and her friendly tongue bobbed back and forth like a shuttle till it had woven the whole intrigue. Gagliuso offered himself, and the king gave him a fat dowry with his daughter.

After a month's merry-making Gagliuso told his royal father-in-law that he wished to carry his bride to his estates. The king accompanied them as far as the frontier, after which they went to Lombardy, where, by the cat's advice, Gagliuso bought a vast domain with the title of baron.

Master Gagliuso, on seeing himself as rich as a prince, thanked the cat in the warmest way imaginable, telling her over and over again that it was to her that he owed his wealth and grandeur. The wit of a cat had done more for him than all his father's sense. She might dispose of the property and life of her dear master as she saw fit. And when she died—would to heaven that she might live a hundred years!—he pledged her his word that he would have her embalmed and put in a golden casket, which he would keep in his chamber, that he might always have her cherished remembrance before his eyes.

The cat was greatly puffed up with all these fine speeches. Before three days had passed, she stretched herself at full length along the garden terrace, pretending to be dead.

"Husband! husband!" cried Gagliuso's wife, "what a great misfortune! The cat is dead!"

"The deuce take her," answered Gagliuso; "better that she should die than we."

"What shall we do with her?" asked the princess.

"Take her by the paw and fling her out of the window."

On hearing this funeral oration, which was not exactly what she was looking for, the cat jumped up, and cried: "So these are your thanks to me for cleansing you of your filth! This is your gratitude for stripping you of rags fit for nothing but a wad for a distaff! This is the way you reward me for feeding you, you scoundrel! for clothing you, you wretch! But it is wasting soap to wash an ass's head. Accursed be all that I have done for you. You are not even worth the trouble of spitting in your face. A fine gold casket you have made ready for me! A splendid funeral you have ordered for me! Well, puss, you have sweated, labored, and worn yourself out, to be paid in such coin! Fool that you were, not to know that service is no inheritance. The philosopher was right who said, 'He who goes to bed an ass will get up an ass.' The more one does, the more one may do. But fine words and foul deeds deceive wise men and fools alike."

With these words she started for the door. Gagliuso followed and attempted in the humblest accents to soften her. His labor was in vain; she would not return, but went straight onward, without turning her head, saying, "Beware of enriching a pauper; he is sure to turn out a villain."

The Priceless Cats

This is an Italian version of the 12th-century British folk tale, *Dick Whittington and His Cat*, with a somewhat different ending.

Among the ancient Romans there was a proverb that those who are greedy never have enough, and since the Romans were Italians, the proverb still holds true. In the golden city of Venice they tell a tale that proves this time-old saying.

There lived in the city by the sea two merchants who were neighbors. Both were rich. Both had grand palaces on the green, shimmering canal, with proud gondolas tied to cinnabar-and-yellow-striped poles. And both had lovely young children who were friendly and played with one another. As for the merchants, one was as different from the other as a black pebble from a shining ruby.

One was hard and sharp and greedy, wanting whatever he saw, whether he needed it or not, while the other was generous and good, working to help not only himself but others as well. The two merchants knew each other and spoke to each other, but when it came to business, Mr. Greedy-Wolf was wary and watchful, not trusting anyone—not even himself.

So time went by, with these two buying and selling, working and growing.

Came a day when Giovanni, the good merchant, set out on a far journey to trade for spices, which were much sought after in Europe then.

He loaded his vessels with toys and corals and silks and beautiful glassware to exchange for pepper and cinnamon and vanilla and curries and other scented spices that grew on the islands far away.

He sailed for days and weeks and then came to the rich East, where he traded from island to island, with benefit to himself and satisfaction to the islanders.

Coles Phillips for the cover of *Good Housekeeping*, April 1914.

One sparkling morning he came to a harbor that was as still as a graveyard, with masts hanging like tombstones. The streets and the markets were quiet as the night.

The merchant and some of his men walked about—disturbed by their own footsteps. Where were the hustling and bustling townspeople dressed in colorful clothes? Where were the smells of spices and the cries of vendors that usually filled the air of a busy city?

Finally the traders from Venice met two men who took them before the King. The ruler sat on his throne with a sorrowful face and head bowed low. Courtiers stood around, no different from the King.

"Can we trade with your people, Your Majesty?" the Venetian merchant said. "We have rich goods from our land that we would gladly exchange for spices."

"Master merchant," said the ruler, "our spices are ravaged, our grain is destroyed, our food is ruined. It is a wonder we are alive, because of the terrible plague that has come over our land. Everything is slowly being destroyed—even our clothes."

"And what is this terrible plague that has brought your land such unhappiness, Your Majesty?"

"Gnawing rats and scuttling mice! They are in our homes and clothes and in our fields and roads. We have set traps for them and we have strewn poison in the pantries, but that has done more harm to our animals than to our pests. There seems to be no remedy for this curse."

"Have you no cats?" the merchant asked.

"Cats? What are cats?"

"Why, cats are furry little animals like small dogs, and they are the mortal enemies of mice and rats, destroying them wherever they find them!"

"Where can I find these cats?" the King cried. "I'll pay anything for them!"

"Your Majesty," Don Giovanni said, "you do not have to pay for cats. We have many of them on our ship, and I will gladly give you a present of some; I am certain your pests will soon be gone."

The King thanked the merchant, almost with tears in his eyes, and within an hour the merchant brought two fine cats—one, a black Tom as fierce as he was big, and the other a lovely tiger-striped lady cat who was famous for having many kittens and catching even more mice.

The King and the islanders looked with awe and wonder at the two animals, for they had never seen cats before, and when they saw them set to work at once on the mice and rats, they were so overjoyed that they wanted to sing and dance.

The King was grateful from the bottom of his heart and wanted to prove this to the merchant, so he showered him and his crew with bales of spices and gleaming jewels, with sweet-smelling sandalwood and carved ivory, beautiful as a song.

When the merchant and his crew sailed home, they were so happy and contented that even the wind and waves knew it and led their vessel swiftly back to Venice.

And the joy of Don Giovanni's family was great when he reached home, and great was the excitement of his fellow merchants of Venice when they saw his royal cargo.

Don Giovanni met Don Cesare, his neighbor, before the golden church of San Marco, that treasury of beauty in the world. They spoke of this and that, about the journey and the trading, and then Don Giovanni told Don Cesare how he had traded the richest merchandise of all for just a pair of common cats. Don Cesare's tongue nearly hung out with greed and envy when they parted.

Thereafter, day and night, Don Cesare could think only of how Don Giovanni had gained a treasure by giving away two worthless cats that any Venetian would pay to get rid of. He had no peace, and he was more restless than a horse with a thorn in his side. Green jealousy and greed ate into him like fire in dry grass, until he could stand it no longer. He had to go to that island and bring back as big, if not a bigger, treasure than had Don Giovanni.

He fitted out a splendid ship filled with the best of goods, golden vessels, brocades, carved corals. With such gifts the generous King should give him twice—no, three times—as many riches as he had given Don Giovanni.

Soon Don Cesare reached the island. He told the King he was

a friend of Don Giovanni. The King received him with open arms, only too happy to welcome a friend of the man who, by his generous gift, had rid the island of the terrible pests.

Don Cesare told the King he, too, had brought him gifts—gifts much more valuable than those of Don Giovanni. Then he presented his gifts of golden cups and carved corals, rich brocades and gilded embroideries—the richest Venice could show to prove his friendship.

Truly the emperor was overwhelmed by this show of unselfish generosity. He was a simple and an honest man, and appreciative as well, and he thought hard how he could repay the friendship shown by Don Cesare. Try as he would, he could think of nothing rich enough and fine enough.

In the end he called together his counsellors to decide what to give to Don Cesare in return for the lavish presents, which, the King thought, Don Cesare had given out of the kindness of his heart.

Each elder had his say. In the end, one rich in wisdom arose and said, "Oh, King, this man from Venice has given to you and to us things that will be a joy to look at for years to come. Truly, we in our little island have no gifts to equal his. We could give him spices and perfumes and woods, but these are simple things growing freely in our land. They come and go every year. But there is one thing we possess now that is of great value in this world. . . ."

. . . the King set a day for the great royal audience to present the merchant with his reward. All the counsellors came, and as many people as the room could hold, and then the merchant appeared before the King. He came with light steps and greedy thought, thinking of the riches he would reap now—riches that would surely be greater than those Don Giovanni had received.

There were blowing of trumpets and beating of drums and many folderal speeches of friendship on the part of the merchant.

In the end the royal master said, "Don Cesare, you came to our land and gave me kindly gifts freely from the goodness of your heart. That is a fine thing for a man to do. And, as the saying goes,

Arthur Rackham (1867–1939). British illustrator.

from seeds of goodness grow rich purple plums of goodness. I and my counsellors thought for a long time how to reward you properly for such unselfish generosity, and finally we decided on the most valuable gift we have.

"When my people and my land were in their greatest distress, a countryman of yours saved us by giving us a gift. It was a gift more precious than gold or diamonds or spices. We have been unable to think of anything more wonderful than the same gift for you. We know it will bring you the same joy and peace it has brought to us. Soldiers, bring the golden cage with the royal gift for Don Cesare!"

Then two soldiers came in with the golden cage in which two little kittens were playing in a way that was a joy to behold.

The soldiers stopped with the cage before the merchant. The King smiled happily, as did the courtiers and the people.

The merchant looked at the kittens, but he could not say a word, and when he saw everyone beaming and smiling at him, he had to smile, too—a smile that stretched from ear to ear. . . . Soon after he sailed homeward.

A Persian cat, from Richard Lydekker's *The New Natural History*, 1890s.

A Persian Tale

ROSE FYLEMAN, from *Forty Good-Morning Tales*, 1929. British author.

James Marabout is my Persian cat. That is only part of his name. His whole name is too long to tell you here. He is very beautiful indeed. He has long silver-grey fur, which, although it is brushed every day, goes into thick-pointed tufts. His little grey nose is slightly curved, like the noses of lovely Persian ladies in pictures. He has large round eyes like pools of amber. The pupils of them are so brightly black that it fascinates one to look at them.

I always knew he wasn't an ordinary cat. Lately he has taken to telling me little stories when we are alone. One day I looked up from my book and said, "Jim, have you ever heard of Rustem?"

Jim looked at me scornfully; his whiskers twitched in the firelight. "Of Rustem," he said, "our great Persian Hero? What do you think?" He blinked his yellow eyes thoughtfully. "I'll tell you a story about him that you won't find in any of your books," he said.

And this is the story:

Once Rustem, who was a brave fighter, saved a magician from some robbers who had fallen upon him suddenly in a lonely place.

Pierre-Auguste Renoir (1841–1919). French painter.

Rustem invited the old man to spend the night in his tent, and after supper they sat outside in the cool air and watched a big fire which Rustem's servants had lighted. It was a clear, starlit night, but there was a quick little breeze fluttering about.

It caught the smoke of the fire so that it danced and whirled about in a thousand queer shapes. The stars seemed to dance with the smoke, they glittered and gleamed between the eddies, and here and there a little tongue of darting flame joined in the dance too. Presently the magician spoke.

"I should like to make thee a gift, Rustem," he said, "in return for what thou hast done for me. What beautiful thing dost thou desire?"

"I desire nothing," said Rustem. "What could be more beautiful than that smoke and the fire and the stars?"

"I will make a gift for thee out of the smoke and the flame and the stars," said the magician.

And he took a handful of smoke and a flame of fire and two bright stars, and kneaded them together for a minute.

"There," he said, "there is thy gift."

Rustem was delighted, for the magician had made a little live creature, soft and grey like the smoke, with bright, star-like eyes and with a little red tongue like a tiny flame of fire. It danced and capered about, and was a joy to look upon.

"Take it home," said the magician. "It will be a plaything for thy children and an ornament to thy house."

And Rustem did so.

"And that," said Jim, "is how the first Persian kitten came into the world. And I ought to know. It was my earliest ancestor."

Sir John Tenniel, 1865. British cartoonist and illustrator.

Alice's Adventures in Wonderland (excerpt)

LEWIS CARROLL, 1865. British storyteller.

So she set the little creature down, and felt quite relieved to see it trot away into the wood. "If it had grown up," she said to herself, "it would have made a dreadfully ugly child: but it makes rather a handsome pig, I think." And she began thinking over other children she knew, who might do very well as pigs, and was just saying to herself "if one only knew the right way to change them—" when she was a little startled by seeing the Cheshire Cat sitting on a bough of a tree a few yards off.

The Cat only grinned when it saw Alice. It looked good-natured, she thought: still it had *very* long claws and a great many teeth, so she felt it ought to be treated with respect.

"Cheshire Puss," she began, rather timidly, as she did not at all know whether it would like the name: however, it only grinned a little wider. "Come, it's pleased so far," thought Alice, and she went on, "Would you tell me, please, which way I ought to walk from here?"

"That depends a good deal on where you want to get to," said the Cat.

"I don't much care where—" said Alice.

"Then it doesn't matter which way you walk," said the Cat.

"—so long as I get *somewhere*," Alice added as an explanation.

"Oh, you're sure to do that," said the Cat, "if you only walk long enough."

Alice felt that this could not be denied, so she tried another question. "What sort of people live about here?"

"In *that* direction," the Cat said, waving its right paw round, "lives a Hatter: and in *that* direction," waving the other paw, "lives a March Hare. Visit either you like: they're both mad."

"But I don't want to go among mad people," Alice remarked.

"Oh, you can't help that," said the Cat: "we're all mad here. I'm mad. You're mad."

"How do you know I'm mad?" said Alice.

"You must be," said the Cat, "or you wouldn't have come here."

Alice didn't think that proved it at all; however, she went on: "and how do you know that you're mad?"

"To begin with," said the Cat, "a dog's not mad. You grant that?"

"I suppose so," said Alice.

"Well then," the Cat went on, "you see a dog growls when it's angry, and wags its tail when it's pleased. Now *I* growl when I'm pleased, and wag my tail when I'm angry. Therefore I'm mad."

"*I* call it purring, not growling," said Alice.

"Call it what you like," said the Cat. "Do you play croquet with the Queen to-day?"

"I should like it very much," said Alice, "but I haven't been invited yet."

"You'll see me there," said the Cat, and vanished.

Alice was not much surprised at this, she was getting so well used to queer things happening. While she was still looking at the place where it had been, it suddenly appeared again.

Sir John Tenniel

"By-the-bye, what became of the baby?" said the Cat. "I'd nearly forgotten to ask."

"It turned into a pig," Alice answered very quietly, just as if the Cat had come back in a natural way.

"I thought it would," said the Cat, and vanished again.

Alice waited a little, half expecting to see it again, but it did not appear and after a minute or two she walked on in the direction in which the March Hare was said to live. "I've seen hatters before," she said to herself: "the March Hare will be much the most interesting, and perhaps as this is May it won't be raving mad—at least not so mad as it was in March." As she said this, she looked up, and there was the Cat again, sitting on a branch of a tree.

"Did you say pig, or fig?" said the Cat.

"I said pig," replied Alice; "and I wish you wouldn't keep appearing and vanishing so suddenly: you make one quite giddy."

"All right," said the Cat; and this time it vanished quite slowly, beginning with the end of the tail, and ending with the grin, which remained some time after the rest of it had gone.

"Well! I've often seen a cat without a grin," thought Alice; "but a grin without a cat! It's the most curious thing I ever saw in all my life!"

Arthur Rackham, from *St. Nicholas*, 1913.

An Old British Fairy Tale

A king and queen who for years had longed for a daughter finally had one born to them. They were the happiest people on earth except for one thing. A year before the princess was born her birth had been predicted along with a warning by a sorceress. It was the warning that weighed heavily on the hearts of the two monarchs.

"Your daughter will fall dead if she ever gives her hand in marriage to a prince," they had been told. "Heed this advice. Find three pure white cats and let them grow up with your child. Give them balls of two types to play with—balls of gold and balls of linen thread. If they ignore the gold and play with the linen, all will be well, but should they ignore the linen and choose the gold, beware!"

The three cats were duly found and became good friends. Better yet they learned to love their young mistress and she them, and as the months passed and became years the linen balls continued to be the only toys the cats chose to play with. The gold balls would have gathered cobwebs had they not been dusted regularly, and everyone began to forget their original purpose.

When the princess grew old enough to learn how to spin the cats were happy as she was. They leaped at the wheel as it turned and at the thread as the princess made it. She begged them to leave things alone but they paid no attention to her and continued to play gaily. The queen, happy as she was in their continued neglect of the gold balls, laughed and indulged their frolicking.

The princess was now 16 years old and very beautiful. People came from far and near to see her beauty, and princes continued to ask for her hand in marriage, but she remained indifferent to all. She seemed perfectly content to continue living as she was with her three beloved cats.

One day, however, a prince arrived who was so good and wise and handsome in her eyes that she knew she would marry him at once if he asked. But although he visited the palace often and brought many gifts he never mentioned the subject of marriage. As he was leaving from one of his extended visits she finally could bear it no longer and confessed her love for him, and he, in delighted surprise, expressed his for her.

The cats were in the tower room playing with the linen balls but no sooner had the prince and princess professed their love for each other, than they seemed to see the gold balls for the first time in their lives and gave chase to them. The news spread throughout the palace but it wasn't the princess who was affected by the switch in balls. The prince became gravely ill and nothing the physicians tried helped to cure the strange malady which had struck him down.

In desperation the princess sought the sorceress who had made the prophecy about the cats and balls. What she learned from her was almost as bad as knowing nothing. There was only one almost impossible way to save the prince. Only 27 days remained before Christmas but in that time she would have to spin 10,000 skeins of pure white linen thread if her lover, whose thread of life had reached the breaking point, would live. No hand but hers could spin the 10,000 skeins and the prince would die at midnight of Christmas night if they weren't finished by then.

The sadly frightened girl rushed home to her spinning wheel and worked steadily until dawn. More discouraged than tired she gazed at the little she had accomplished and burst into tears. Through her sobs she seemed to hear her cats call to her.

Ready to believe anything she gazed lovingly at them. "If you only knew what was wrong I know you'd help me if you could," she told them.

"We know what's needed and can and will help you," they replied. "After all, we don't have hands but paws so we can do the spinning for you and no one will be able to object. Now please let us get to work. Even for us the time left is very short."

And so it was that the three cats began to spin, each at a wheel provided for it. And spin they did—rapidly and beautifully. All day the three wheels hummed and when they were silent as evening came the princess looked into the room to find her beloved cats sound asleep next to 300 skeins of thread.

As the days passed and the skeins grew in number the prince's health began to mend and the princess's spirits soared. On Christmas day the 10,000 skeins were ready for the sorceress and the prince was almost well.

The sorceress was more than pleased with the cats' work and told the princess to be sure and show her gratitude to the cats for saving the life of her lover. Such a reminder was unnecessary. The girl had always loved them as much as she thought possible but her gratitude had increased even this great love. She gave them all her jewels which she found they had always greatly admired, and at the

Julie Manet with a Cat, Pierre-Auguste Renoir, 1887. French painter.

wedding feast, decked in these jewels, they sat in a place of honor on magnificent cushions.

As the feast continued the cats curled up contentedly on their cushions and suddenly from all three came a pleasant hum. It was the wonderful, happy sound of purring, the reward, the cats explained to the princess, they had received for their help to her. Strangely enough the sound was very much like the whir and hum of a spinning wheel. And from that day to this cats have continued to purr whenever they feel contented.

CHAPTER 8

Coronation in the Valley of Gods

The Perfected Soul saith: ". . . I am the greatest cat which dwelleth in the seat of right and truth wherein riseth the god Shu."

What then is this? The male cat is Ra himself, and he is called Maau. . . .

The Egyptian Book of the Dead, ca. 1500 B.C.

Like those great sphinxes lounging through eternity in noble attitudes upon the desert sand, they gaze incuriously at nothing, calm and wise.

Charles Baudelaire (1821–1867).

To many people cats are quite special. Some civilizations have even taken their reverence of cats to the point of worship. Both the Peruvians and the Chinese had agricultural gods in the form of cats. The Peruvian god of fertility and healing, Ai Apaec, had the form of an old man/ tomcat. The Chinese believed that all cats had the ability to see in the dark. Their cat deity, Li Shou, warded off evil spirits, which were more active at night. The chariot of Freyja, the Scandinavian fertility goddess, was drawn by cats. Farmers would leave offerings for Freyja's cats, to ensure good crops and protection against bad weather. The Roman goddess Diana sometimes assumed the shape of a cat. She was the goddess of the forest and of childbirth.

The Egyptians' reverence for cats is probably the most famous. Mafdet was their first cat deity, reigning from 2500 to 2280 B.C. Nut, the sky goddess, occasionally was represented with the head of a cat, and Ra, the sun god, was sometimes referred to as the Great Cat. Even though most Egyptians were vegetarians and therefore did not kill animals, occasionally they sacrificed cats to their cat gods and sometimes used cats in casting spells.

Bast (Bastet or Pascht) is the most well-known of the Egyptian cat-headed goddesses. She was worshipped as the goddess of fire and the personification of the moon from before 1780 B.C. to A.D. 392, when her cult was banned by imperial decree. At her city, Bubastis, all cats were considered divine. The temples were full of them, and they were cared for by a special group of priestesses. Each spring 700,000 worshippers converged on Bubastis for one of the liveliest festivals of the year.

The Egyptian's devotion occasionally was used against them. In 525 B.C. the Egyptian port of Pelusia came under seige by Cambyses, the Persian king and son of Cyrus the Great. He ordered his 600 soldiers to strap live cats to their shields and to storm the walls of the city. When the Egyptians saw the cats, they immediately stopped fighting and surrendered. They refused to take the chance that even one cat might be harmed.

When Egyptian cats died, they were brought to certain cities to be mummified and prepared for life in the afterworld. Mice were left near the mummies for the cats to eat on awakening. In 1888 an estimated 300,000 mummified cats were found at Beni Hassan. They were scooped up with tractors, sold at the price of $18.43 per ton, and sent to England where they were ground up for fertilizer. The cat mummies weren't alone in this irreverent treatment. Millions of human mummies were used as fuel for locomotives in Egypt in the late 19th century.

During the 17th century in Turkey, cats were treated with the same consideration as children. Distinguished citizens set up foundations to support cats. The cats could live independently if they wanted to and special houses were established where they could spend the night.

A Varied Life (excerpt)

GENERAL SIR THOMAS EDWARD GORDON, 1906. British officer.

For twenty-five years an oral addition to the written standing orders of the native guard at Government House near Poona had been communicated regularly from one guard to another on relief, to the effect that any cat passing out of the front door after dark was to be regarded as His Excellency, the Governor, and to be saluted accordingly. The meaning of this was that Sir Robert Grant, Governor of Bombay, had died there in 1838 and on the evening of the day of his death a cat was seen to leave the house by the front door

Alexandre Desportes (1661–1743).

and walk up and down a particular path, as it had been the Governor's habit to do after sunset. A Hindu sentry had observed this, and he mentioned it to others of his faith, who made it a subject of superstitious conjecture, the result being that one of the priestly class explained the mystery of the dogma of the transmigration of the soul from one body to another, and interpreted the circumstance to mean that the spirit of the deceased Governor had entered into one of the house pets.

It was difficult to fix on a particular one, and it was therefore decided that every cat passing out of the main entrance after dark was to be treated with due respect and the proper honours. The decision was accepted without question by all the native attendants and others belonging to Government House. The whole guard, from sepoy to sibadar, fully acquiesced to it, and an oral addition was made to the standing orders that the sentry at the front door "present arms to any cat passing out there after dark."

Gospel of the Holy Twelve

(three excerpts)

Received in visions by Reverend G. J. Ousley in 1923, who claims it to be the translation of an early Christian document that was hidden by the Essenes in a Buddhist monastery in Tibet.

And there were in the same cave an ox and a horse and an ass and a sheep, and beneath the manger was a cat with her little ones; and there were doves also overhead; and each had its mate after its kind, the male with the female.

Thus it came to pass that He was born in the midst of the animals which, through redemption of man from ignorance and selfishness, He came to redeem from their sufferings by the manifestation of the Son of God.

As Jesus passed through a certain village He saw a crowd of idlers of the baser sort, and they were tormenting a cat which they had found and shamefully treating it. And Jesus commanded them to desist, and began to reason with them.

And as Jesus entered into a certain village He saw a young cat which had none to care for her, and she was hungry and cried unto Him; and He took her up, and put her inside His garment, and she lay in His bosom.

And when He came into the village He set food and drink before the cat, and she ate and drank, and shewed thanks unto Him. And He gave her unto one of His disciples who was a widow, whose name was Lorenza, and she took care of her.

And one of those who were with Him said, "Behold, this man loveth all creatures. How is it that He loveth all living things as if they were His brothers and sisters?"

And Jesus said, "Verily I say unto ye, these creatures are children of God even as ye are, and are indeed your brethren and sis-

Study for *Madonna with the Cat*, Leonardo da Vinci (1452–1519). Italian painter, sculptor, architect, engineer.

ter. And whoso giveth them food and drink giveth it to Me. And whoso doeth them harm or doth not protect them, harmeth Me and doth not protect Me."

The Cousin of Mahomet (excerpt)

This account is based on the 7th-century story of the Islamic prophet Mohammed (A.D. 567–632) and his cat Muezza. Mohammed's love for his cat is said to have made the cat a sacred animal for Muslims.

Turkish women are not very fond of Mohammedan doctrine, and do not feel obliged to obey the commands of a man who preferred his cat to them, giving the cat a place in paradise from which the women are excluded. They don't know, or pretend not to know that this venerable cat was a "virtusos," i.e., a holy person. Here is an episode of his history. The prophet's puss was one day lying on the sleeve of his master's coat, in such deep meditation on a point of the law that Mahomet, whose time to pray had come, and not daring to interrupt his ecstasy, cut off his sleeve so as not to disturb him. On his return, his cat had awoken from his ecstatic slumber, and had seen the sleeve which Mahomet had cut off for him, and recognized Mahomet's good intention.

The cat rose to do him reverence, raised his tail and arched his back to express more respect. Mahomet, understanding perfectly the meaning of this, accorded this saintly cat a place in Paradise. Then, stroking his back three times, he gave him, by this laying on of hands, the power of never falling on to this region, whence comes the fact that cats always land on their feet. I have often heard venerable Turks tell quite seriously this story, which it would be dangerous to make fun of in their presence.

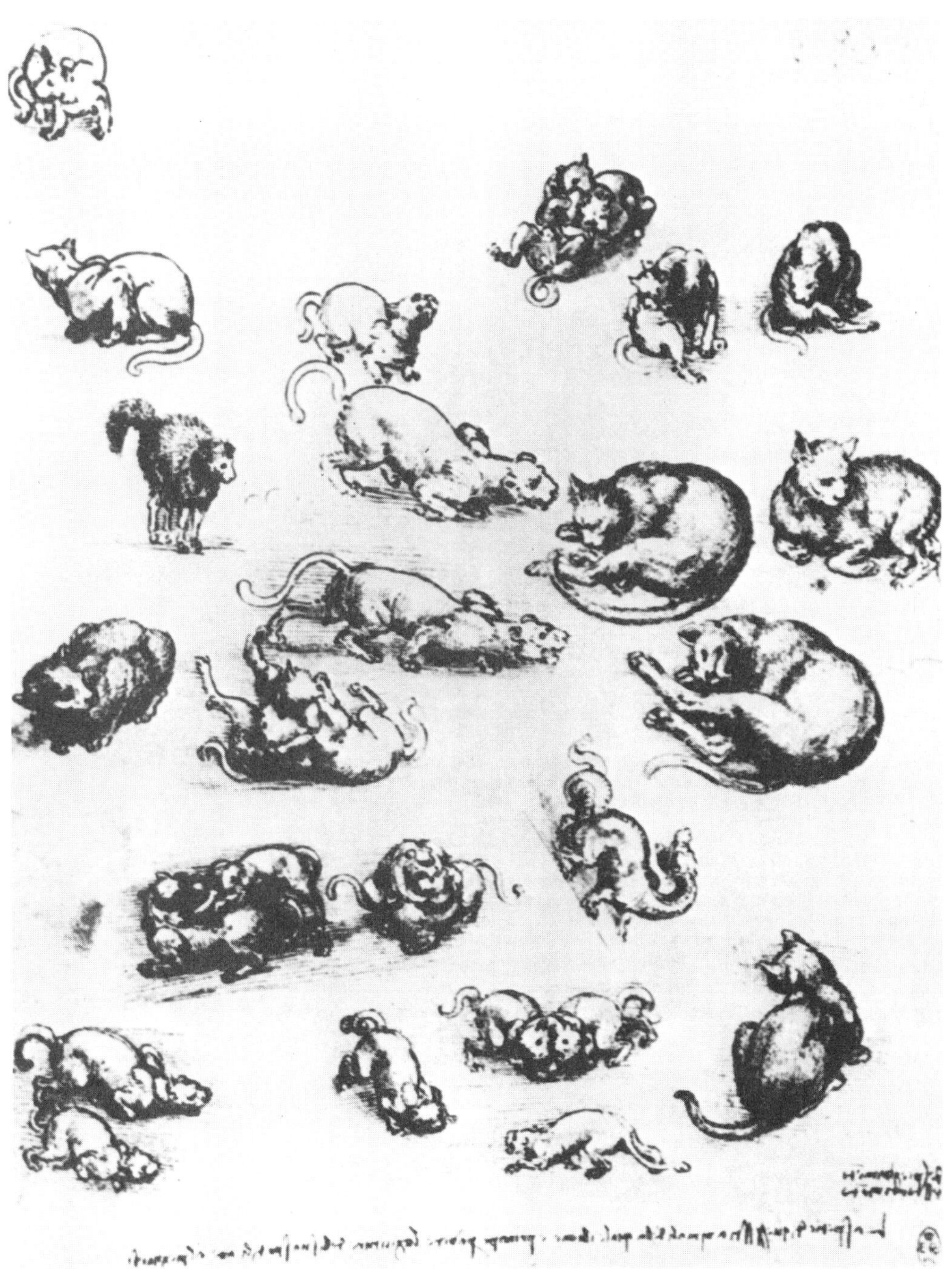

Studies of cats, Leonardo da Vinci (1452–1519). Italian painter, sculptor, architect, engineer.

Bibliotheke (excerpt)

DIODORUS SICULUS, ca. 30 B.C. Roman historian.

Whoever kills a cat in Egypt is condemned to death, whether he committed this crime deliberately or not. The people gather and kill him. An unfortunate Roman, who had accidentally killed a cat, could not be saved, either by King Ptolemy of Egypt or by the fear which Rome inspired.

Every night Ra, the sun god (depicted as the cat), would engage in a cosmic battle with serpent Apophis, the god of darkness and chaos. Ra is shown killing Apophis in this Egyptian papyrus, *The Papyrus of Ani, The Egyptian Book of the Dead*, ca. 1500 B.C.

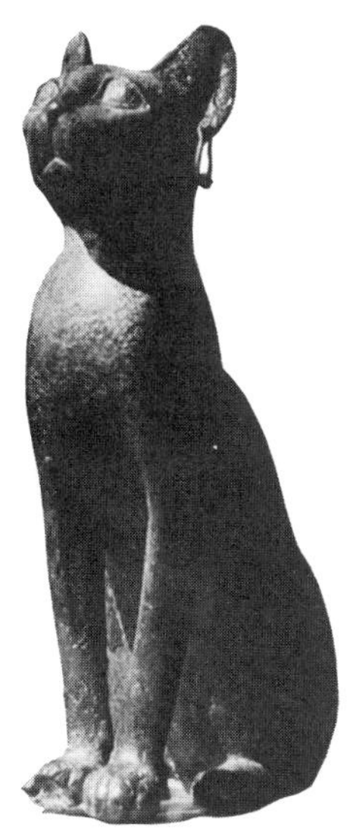

Egyptian bronze statue of a cat, ca. 600 B.C.

(Untitled)

Two Egyptologists writing about the life of cats in the Nile valley.

Cats were the living representation of their household gods; they indeed are like gods in that they receive affection without returning it, there is in them something unearthly and mysterious. They see at night as well as by day, and their bright eyes seem to reflect stars. Their whole body contains a light which appears in the dark when their backs are stroked. Therefore the symbolism of the Egyptians gave the head of a she-cat or of a lioness and phosphorescent eyes to Bubastis, incarnation of the brightness which does not come from the sun, luminous goddess of the night. Cats are therefore sacred to her. Thus the priests divided their attention between the statue of Pascht and the tribe of cats which climbed on the alters or slept in the lap of the goddess. Every action, every movement of these fortunate animals was commented on, and oracles were based on their friskings and mewings, as in other places on the flight of the ibis or the vulture. The priests of Pascht were the first to predict rain when the cats passed their paws over their ears.

The arrangement of mummies suggests that there was a strict hierarchy among cats. Some were swathed in strips of cloth covered with hieroglyphics praising them, and buried alone; whole groups of others were embalmed together and enclosed in a single covering. The coat, its colour, the cat's age and no doubt other factors determined no doubt the extent of the honours due to each.

Enterpé (excerpt)

HERODOTUS, ca. 430 B.C. Greek historian.

Egypt, though it borders upon Libya, is not a region abounding in wild animals. The animals that do exist in the country, whether domesticated or otherwise, are all regarded as sacred. If I were to explain why they are consecrated to the several gods, I should be led to speak of religious matters, which I particularly shrink from mentioning; the points whereon I have touched slightly hitherto have all been introduced from sheer necessity. Their custom with respect to animals is as follows: —For every kind there are appointed certain guardians, some male, some female, whose business it is to look after them; and this honour is made to descend from father to son. The inhabitants of the various cities, when they have made a vow to any god, pay it to his animals

Egyptian papyrus.

A cat on a leash, Egyptian papyrus, ca. 2600 B.C.

in the way which I will now explain. At the time of making the vow they shave the head of the child, cutting off all the hair, or else half, or sometimes a third part, which they then weigh in a balance against a sum of silver; and whatever sum the hair weighs is presented to the guardian of the animals, who thereupon cuts up some fish, and gives it to them for food—such being the stuff whereon they are fed. When a man has killed one of the sacred animals, if he did it with malice prepense, he is punished with death, if unwittingly, he has to pay such a fine as the priests choose to impose. When an ibis, however, or a hawk is killed, whether it was done by accident or on purpose the man must needs die.

The number of domestic animals in Egypt is very great, and would be still greater were it not for what befalls the cats. As the females, when they have kittened, no longer seek the company of the males, these last, to obtain once more their companionship, practice a curious artifice. They seize the kittens, carry them off, and kill them, but do not eat them afterwards. Upon this the females, being deprived of their young, and longing to supply their place, seek the males once more, since they are particularly fond of their off-spring.

If a fire breaks out in an Egyptian house, the people pay little attention to the fire and think only of their cats. They surround and guard them, and if by mischance one of the cats runs into the flames, the Egyptians are heartbroken. (In this case, the women blacken their faces and run through the streets in a state of utter grief.)

If a cat dies of sickness or old age, all the people of the house cut off their eyebrows. The magistrates come with ceremony to collect the body, which is embalmed with fragrant oils, cedar, and other aromatic compounds to preserve it. It is then brought to Bubast, to be buried there in a temple. The dogs are interred in the cities to which they belong, also in sacred burial-places. The same practice obtains with respect to the ichneumons; the hawks and shrew-mice, on the contrary, are conveyed to the city of Buto for burial, and the ibises to Hermopolis. The bears, which are scarce in Egypt, and the wolves, which are not much bigger than foxes, they bury wherever they happen to find them lying.

Votive Stela

Top inscription: "The Great Cat, the Peaceful One is his good name, he who belongs to Atum at rest. The Good Cat . . . of Ra."

Bottom inscription (prayer): "Giving adoration to the Great Cat, kissing the earth [for] the herald of Ra, the peaceful one who has returned to rest. . . . Reveal to me the vision of your beauty, then peacefully brightness shall return to me. I shall be at peace, knowing [your] beauty. May you give life, prosperity, and health to the soul of. . . ."

1558–1085 B.C., found at Deir el Medineh. The top panel depicts bread and vegetable offerings between two cats. The bottom shows the stela's owner and his wife, their left hands raised in adoration, and has a prayer with blanks left for the owner's name to be inserted.

Bast

WILLIAM ROSE BENÉT (1886–1950). American poet, novelist, and editor.

She had green eyes, that excellent seer,
And little peaks to either ear.
She sat there, and I sat here.

She spoke of Egypt, and a white
Temple, against enormous night.

She smiled with clicking teeth and said
That the dead were never dead;

Said old emperors hung like bats
In barns at night, or ran like rats—
But empresses came back as cats!

An Egyptian statue of Bast, 600–200 B.C.

CHAPTER 9

Sorcery from the Netherworld

Yet before she departed, the Witch desired the maid to live with her, and she would teach her a more stranger Art: What's that, said the maid, she answered, you shall know presently, and forthwith she appeared in the shape of a great black Cat, and lay along by the Chimney.

An account of the trial of Anne Bodenham written in 1653.

"What's the matter with the cat? . . . Look at her!" "Mad, I think. And no wonder in this evil place."

Charles Dickens, *Bleak House*, 1853.

When people think of witches, they often think of cats. The association of cats with witchcraft began with the Catholic church's persecution of religious groups, some of whom worshipped the cat. In the 12th century this persecution spread to splinter groups of the church itself, such as the Cathars, whom the church accused of worshipping the Devil in the form of a cat. This led to stories of Satan's appearing at Black Masses as a cat.

The witch trials started in the 13th century. People began to believe that witches had the ability to turn into an animal, usually a hare or a cat, in order to transport themselves to a sabbat (a midnight meeting) presided over by the Devil. This idea was still popular in 1718, when it was recorded that at Caithness, Scotland, a man named William Montgomery thought he heard cats gossiping in human voices outside his house. Armed with a sword and a hatchet, he rushed out and killed two cats and wounded others. The next morning two local women were found dead and the leg of a third was so badly wounded it withered and fell off.

It was believed that a witch could transform another witch into a cat by saying, "The Devil speed thee and go thou with me." The 1584 book *Beware of the Cat* said that a witch could only take the form of a cat nine times, nine being a mystical number (a trinity of trinities) and the number of lives of a cat.

The idea of familiar spirits soon developed. These were imps or minor demons who took the form of any small animal, from a hedgehog to a toad. A familiar acted as an intermediary for the witch, carrying out her orders so that she wouldn't have to be at the scene of the crime when the evil deed was done.

A witch's cat came to be called a grimalkin. The Scottish goddess of witches was called Mither o' the Mawkins, a mawkin or malkin being either a cat or a hare. Originally a greymalkin was a gray cat. Later the term came to refer to the "pussies" or "catkins" on a pussy willow, as well as to the witch's cat.

The Black Death devastated Europe from 1346 to 1349. This and other plagues were blamed on witchcraft, and the witch trials became intense at this time. Pope Innocent VIII issued a decree in 1484 denouncing all cats and anyone who owned one. He commanded that, whenever a witch was burned, her cats must be burned with her. Inquisitor Nicholas Remy echoed this a century later when he said that all cats were demons. During this period priests presided over festivals where cats were burned by the hundreds.

With acute labor shortages caused by the plagues, landowners turned to less labor-intensive activities, such as sheep farming. For the poor, food and jobs became scarce. As economic problems grew, the witch trials offered an excuse to get rid of "economically useless" old women. Women such as these, isolated from society, had turned to their cats for friendship.

In Europe and Britain over 200,000 supposed witches were executed. Handbooks for magistrates in the 1600s insisted that possession of a familiar—a cat—was the primary evidence of witchcraft. In New England there were over 2000 cat-related witch trials. Millions of cats were destroyed, and the species was brought to the point of extinction.

Stanley L. Wood, from *Dr. Nikola*, 1896.

Dr. Faustus to His Cats

ANNE YOUNG, from *Saturday Review*, 1951. American poet.

Ah, stay, Grimalkin, flatter me to my doom;
Steal like a shadow in this somber room,
Enrich its fateful silence with thy purr,
Spurn not my restless hand upon thy fur
Dowered with youth for which I, fool, once gave
My all in all. Thou goest bright and brave
Locked, whiskered, at an age would turn to ashes
The golden curls of Helen; thine eye flashes
Like a lanthorn still; gay is thy sport
If grandson or if grandsire pay thee court.

Malkin, we serve one master, blackavised,
The Prince of Darkness. Oft have I surmised
Why the All-loving spake to thee in ire:
"Go seek a nook beside the quenchless fire,
Nor pray a shelter in the Heavenly house."
Did He behold thy way with bird or mouse
Trembling between thy paws? But thou didst sin
After thy nature only, I within
My sacred soul, and thus eternity
Measures my doom, while one far day may see
Thee sated with Hell creep home a prodigal
To the Father's feet, and there thy prey let fall
Unscathed, a wistful prayer in thy soft miaou
To win His smile of welcome. Even now
Satan adores thee whom he cannot hold
While me scorns safe pent within his fold.
So variously, Grimalkin, we are undone:
Thy portion cream, mine nightshade, of the Evil One.

Old Judy, the Witch of Burwell

A rhyme from the 1880s.

A wicked old crone
Who lived all alone
In a hut beside the reeds
With a high crowned hat
And a black tom-cat,
Whose looks were as black as her deeds.

A witch and her cat, 1856.

The Old Woman and Her Cats

JOHN GAY (ca. 1685–1732). British poet.

A wrinkled Hag, of wicked fame,
Beside a little smoky flame
Sat hov'ring, pinch'd with age and frost;
Her shrivell'd hands, with veins embossed,
Upon her knees her weight sustain,
While palsy shook her crazy brain:
She mumbles forth her backward pray'rs,
An untam'd scold of fourscore years.
About her swarm'd a num'rous brood
Of Cats, who lank with hunger mew'd.
Teased with their cries, her choler grew,
And thus she sputter'd: Hence, ye crew.
Fool that I was, to entertain
Such imps, such fiends, a hellish train!

A witch and her cat, by
F. H. Townsend, 1913.

Had ye been never hous'd and nurs'd,
I, for a witch, had ne'er been curs'd.
To you I owe, that crowds of boys
Worry me with eternal noise;
Straws laid across, my pace retard;
The horse-shoe's nail'd (each threshold's guard)
The stunted broom the wenches hide,
For fear that I should up and ride. . . .

'Tis infamy to serve a hag;
Cats are thought imps, her broom a nag;
And boys against our lives combine,
Because, 'tis said, your cats have nine.

Testimony of the Witches of Chelmsford

Testimony from the first witch trial in which a cat played a major role.

The Examination and confession of certain Wytches at Chensford in the Countie of Essex before the Quenes maiesties Judges, the xxvi daye of July Anno 1556 At the Assise holden there as then, and one of them put to death for the same offence, as their examination declareth more at large.

The examination of them with their confession before Doctor Cole and master Foscue at the same Sise verbatum, as nere as coulde be gathered, and firste of Elizabeth Frauncis who saide as here foloweth.

Fyrst she learned this arte of witchcraft at the age of xii yeres of hyr grandmother, whose nam mother Eue of Hatfyelde Peurell, disseased. Item when shee taughte it her, she counseiled her to renounce GOD and His Worde and to geue of her bloudde to Sathan (as she termed it) wyche she delyuered her in the lykenesse of a whyte spotted Catte, and taughte her to feede the sayde Catte with breade and mylke, and she dyd so, also she taughte her to cal it by the name of Sathan and to kepe it in a basket.

When this mother Eue had geuen her the Cat Sathan, then this Elizabeth desired firste of the sayde Cat (callinge it Sathan) that she might be ryche and to haue goodes, and he promised her she shoulde—askinge her what she would haue . . . (for this Cat spake to her as she confessed in a straunge holowe voice, but such as she vnderstode by vse). . . .

When shee had kept this Cat by the space of xv or xvi yeare, and as some saye (though vntruly) beinge wery of it, she came to one mother Waterhouse her neyghbour (a pore woman) when she was going to the oven and desired her to geue her a cake, and she wold geue her a thing that she should be the better for so long as she liued, and this mother Waterhouse gaue her a cake, where vpon she brought her this cat in her apron and taught her as she was instructed by her grandmother Eue, telling her that she must cal him Sathan, and geue him of her bloude and breade and milke as before, and at this examination woulde confesse no more.

Ensayos (Trials), Francisco José de Goya y Lucientes, 1797–1798. Spanish painter.

Mother Waterhouse of Hatfylde peuerell of the age of lxiiii yeares being examined the same day confessed as followeth, and the xxix daye suffered.

Fyrst she receyued this cat of this Frances wife in the order as is before sayde, who wild her to cal him Sathan, and told her that yf she make muche of him he would do for her what she wolde haue him to do.

Then when she had receyued him she (to trye him what he coulde do) wyld him to kyll a hog of her owne, which he dyd, and she gaue him for his labour a chicken, which he fyrste required of her and a drop of her blod. And this she gaue him at all times when he dyd anythynge for her, by pricking her hand or face and putting the bloud to hys mouth wyche he sucked, and forthwith wold lye downe in hys pot againe wherein she kepte him, the spots of all the which priks are yet to be sene in her skin.

Also she saythe that another tyme being offended with one Father Kersye she toke her catte Sathan in her lap and put hym in the wood before her dore, and willed him to kyll three of this father Kersyes hogges, whiche he dyd, and retourning agayne told her so, and she rewarded hym as before, wyth a chicken and a droppe of her bloud, which chicken he eate vp cleane as he didde al the rest, and she cold fynde remaining neyther bones nor fethers.

Also she confessed that falling out with one widdow Gooday she wylled Sathan to drowne her cow and he dyd so, and she rewardid hym as before.

Also she falling out wyth another of her neyboures, she killed her three geese in the same maner.

Item, shee confessed that because she could haue no rest (which she required) she caused Sathan to destroye the brewing at that tyme.

Also beying denyed butter of an other, she caused her to lose the curdes ii or iii dayes after.

Item fallinge out with an other neybours and his wife, shee wylled Sathan to kyll him with a bludye flixe, whereof he dyed, and she rewarded him as before.

The Dream of Reason Produces Monsters, Francisco José de Goya y Lucientes, 1797. Spanish painter.

Likewyse shee confessed, that because she lyued somwhat vnquietly with her husbande, she caused Sathan to kyll him, and he doid so about ix yeres past, syth which tyme she hath lyued a widdow.

Also she said that when she wolde wyl him to do any thynge for her, she wolde say her Pater noster in laten.

Item, this mother Waterhouse confessed that shee fyrst turned this Cat into a tode by this meanes, she kept the cat a great while in woll in a pot, and at length being moued by pouertie to occupie the woll, she praied in the name of the father and of the sonne and of the holy ghost that it wolde turne into a tode and forthwith it was turned into a tode, and so kept it in the pot without woll.

Also she said, that going to Brackstede a lyttle before her apprehentyon, this Sathan wylled her to hye her home, for she shulde haue great trouble and that shee shoulde be eyther hanged or burned shortly, more at this tyme she woulde not confesse.

Dr. Fain and his Coven at North Berwick, ca. 1800s.

Newes from Scotland (excerpt)

AUTHOR UNKNOWN, 1591.

John Fain, alias Cunninghame, master of the school at Saltpans, Lothian, ever nearest to the devil, at his left elbow . . . chases a cat in Tranent. In which chase he was carried high above the ground, with great swiftness, and as lightly as the cat herself, over a higher dyke. Asked to what effect he chased the creature, he answered that in a conversation held at Brumhoillis, Satan commanded all that were present to take cats: like as he, for obedience to Satan, chased the said cat, to raise winds for destruction of ships and boats.

Criminal Trials in Scotland (excerpt)

ROBERT PITCAIRN, 1833. An account of the 1591 attempt to kill King James VI by using a cat and black magic to sink the king's ship. A storm was raised and the ship was sunk but the king wasn't on it.

And within eight days after the said Bill was delivered, the said Agnes Sampson, Janet Campbell, Johnne Fean, Gelie Duncan, and Meg Dyn baptised one cat in the Wobstars house, in manner following: First, Two of them held one finger, in the one side of the chimney-crook, and one other held one other finger in the other side, the two tips of the fingers meeting together; then they put the cat thrice through the links of the crook, and passed it thrice under the chimney. Thereafter, at Begie Todd's house, they knit to the four feet of the cat, four joints of men; which being done, the said Janet fetched it to Leith; and about midnight, she and the two Linkhop, and two wives called Stobbes, came to the Pierhead and saying their words, "See that there be no deceit amongst us"; and they cast the cat in the sea, so far as they might, which swam over and came again; and they that were in the Panis, cast in one other cat in the sea at eleven o'clock. After which, be there sorcery and enchantment, the boat perished between Leith and Kinghorne.

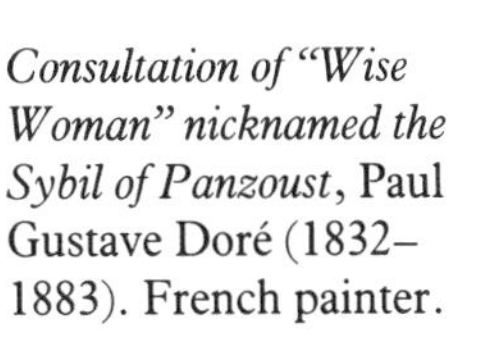

Consultation of "Wise Woman" nicknamed the Sybil of Panzoust, Paul Gustave Doré (1832–1883). French painter.

Compendium Maleficarum (excerpt)

BROTHER FRANCESCO MARIA GUAZZO, 1608. Writer and scholar of the Roman Catholic church.

A certain day-labourer named Philip bore witness in this very city of Ferrara to this apparent conversion of witches into cats. For he swore to me on oath that, three months before, a certain witch had told him not to drive them away if he saw any cats come coying playfully up to his son, whom she had strongly bewitched and had undertaken to cure. The same day, about an hour after she had gone away, he and his wife saw a big cat which they had never seen before go deliberately up to the boy. They were frightened and kept driving it off, and were at last goaded to exasperation by its insistence, and the man shut the door and chased it about for a long time, striking it with a stick, until finally he made it jump out of a high window, so that the cat's body seemed to be all bruised and

Woodblock print from *Compendium Maleficarum*. 1608.

broken. After that, the old witch kept to her bed for many days with a bruised and broken body. Consequently, where there had already been a slight suspicion that she was a witch and had bewitched the boy who lay very sick under the spell of his infirmity, this now grew into a strong and grave suspicion; for the blows and wounds which were given to the cat were found upon the corresponding parts of the witch's body.

Remy writes that nearly all those who came into his hands charged with witchcraft told him that they changed themselves into cats whenever they wished to enter other people's houses in secret, so that they could scatter their poison there by night. Barbelline Rayel, at Blainville-la-Grande on the 1st January, 1587, confessed that she was turned into a cat so that in that shape she might more easily enter the house of Jean Louis and wander about it in greater safety; and when she had done so and found his two-year-old infant unguarded she dusted it with a drugged powder which she held in the pad of her paw, and killed it.

Discours des Sorciers (excerpt)

HENRY BOGUET, 1590. The chief judge of the county of Burgundy, France.

Others have been changed into cats. In our own time one named Charcot of the bailiwick of Gez was attacked by night in a wood by a number of cats; but when he made the sign of the Cross they all vanished. And more recently a horseman was passing by the Chateau de Joux and saw several cats up a tree: he approached and discharged a carbine which he was carrying, thereby causing a ring with several keys attached to it to fall from the tree. These he took to the village, and when he asked for dinner at the inn, neither the hostess nor the keys of the cellar could be found. He showed the bunch of keys which he was carrying, and the host recognised them as his wife's, who meanwhile came up, wounded in the right hip. Her husband seized her, and she confessed that she had just come from the Sabbat, where she had lost her keys after having been wounded in the hip by a shot from a carbine.

The Inquisitors also tell that in their time there were seen three large cats near the town of Strasbourg, which afterwards resumed the shape of women.

19th-century depiction of a witches' sabbat.

The Woman Who Became a Cat, J. J. Grandville (1803–1847). French illustrator.

How to Change into a Cat

ISOBEL GOWDIE, a confessed Scottish witch who was burned in 1665, revealed the spell used to change into a cat and to change back again. Each incantation should be repeated three times.

To change into a cat:

I shall goe intill ane catt,
With sorrow, and sych, and a blak shott;
And I sall goe in the Divellis nam,
Ay will I com hom againe.

To change back into a human:

Catt, catt, God send thee a blak shott.
I am in a cattis liknes just now,
Bot I sal be in a womanis liknes ewin now.
Catt, catt, God send thee a blak shott.

The Witch of Walkerne

ELIZA LYNN LINTON, from *Witchcraft in England*, 1861. English novelist and journalist. On the 1712 witchcraft trial of Jane Wenham.

Moreover, two veracious witnesses deposed positively to her taking the form of a cat when she would, and to hearing her converse with the devil when under the form of a cat, he also as a cat; together with Anne Thorne's distinct accusation that she was beset with cats—tormented exceedingly—and that all the cats had the face and the voice of Jane Wenham.

The lawyers, who believed little in the devil and less in witchcraft, refused to draw up the indictment on any other charge save that of "conversing familiarly with the devil in the form of a cat." But in spite of Mr Bragge's earnest appeals against such profanation, and the ridicule which it threw over the whole matter, the jury found the poor old creature guilty, and the judge passed sentence of death against her. The evidence was too strong. . . . The jury could not resist the tremendous weight of all this evidence, and the judge could not resist the jury, he managed to get a reprieve which left the people time to cool and reflect, and then he got a pardon for her—quietly and kindly done. And Colonel Plummer, of Gilston, took her under his protection, and gave her a small cottage near his house, where she lived, poor soul, in peace and safety to the end of her days, doing harm to no one and feared by none.

From *Historie of Foure-Footed Beastes*, Edmund Topsell, 1658.

An old occult-related symbol.

The Heathens (excerpt)

WILLIAM HOWELLS, 1948. American anthropologist.

Zande (African native) witches are also associated with cats in a loose way. Some female witches may have cat daughters or cat familiars, and may kill people simply by showing the cats to them. However, it seems that the cats are feared in their own right, because people will fall deathly ill at the mere sight of a certain species of bush cat, and on hearing a cat cry they will rush to blow their anti-cat whistles, and sit near their anti-cat plants, which grow in every homestead. Even people of royal blood, who are immune to witchcraft, die of cats, and sudden deaths among them are believed to be from this cause. It is interesting that witches and cats are here feared for the same reason without being bound together as firmly as in the lore of Europe.

The Witch's Cat

MARION WEINSTEIN, 1975. Author, radio show host, and practicing witch.

The cat has often served in the role of witch's familiar. A familiar is a non-human creature that helps the witch in most magic and occult work. The role of familiar goes far beyond the role of a pet animal, because the familiar is both helper and companion to the witch; it is considered an equal.

The cat has always been a favorite choice for a familiar; this tradition can be traced back to the ancient Egyptian mystery schools, in which cats were revered for their psychic powers. Actually, the familiar can be an invisible being or any small animal (toad, mouse, rabbit, small dog, etc.), but cats are particularly good familiars. They have all the qualities that a witch could ever hope to find in an animal helper. A familiar is never "trained;" it must meet the witch on equal ground. Any cat who becomes a familiar inevitably does so of its own free will. It literally volunteers for the work. This is very important in witchcraft, a field of occult work where there is so much emphasis on free will. An independent spirit and voluntary contribution are the only kinds of help a witch can use from an animal.

The witch's work includes E.S.P., telepathy and spirit contact. Cats have a natural talent in all these areas. When a cat wants to read your mind, it can usually do so. Have you ever thought about stepping into the kitchen for a snack and suddenly found your cat at your side? This is not "coincidence" (especially if you're in the habit of giving the cat a handout when you eat something). The cat has actually picked up the image of food from your thoughts. This talent is handy for witches, who often work through their minds. Some things must be said in images and cats have a natural talent for picking up these images.

Furthermore, cats are not afraid of the unseen world, nor are they afraid of unseen beings. Not only are cats unafraid of spirits, but they usually *like* them. Even in non-witch homes I have seen

From *The Ingoldsby Legends*, 1907, Arthur Rackham. British illustrator.

many a cat staring intently at a portrait of someone who has departed this life. Haunted houses are often frequented—or inhabited—by cats. And mediums often attest that they cannot keep their cats out of the room during a séance; in fact, even neighboring cats have been known to show up, eagerly, the moment that lights are dimmed and the table, or ouija board, is set up. This affinity helps not only the witch but any participating spirits. Spirits like to feel welcome when they enter this plane, and when a cat is present and happy to see them, the contact is easier and more friendly for all concerned.

Witches have been misunderstood and persecuted for centuries; whenever they went anywhere, they had to be careful. Their lives were often in danger, and the silent cat made an ideal traveling companion. A witch who went out—to a meeting, on an herb-gathering expedition or simply for a stroll—would find herself in trouble if her comings and goings were heralded by a noisy pet.

Another advantage of the cat's role as familiar is that occult work is traditionally done at night. When the rest of the world is sleeping, one's psychic energies are least likely to be disturbed. Cats are usually wide awake and energetic at night, so they can join right in on the work with ease.

Witches respect all the animal kingdom. They are interested in what is going on in nature. Animals know about approaching weather conditions, impending dangers, the approach of storms, floods and fires. In the days before radio and television, it was especially important to be in contact with these natural forces, to know about them beforehand. The cat was an excellent helper in this area because of its telepathic talent—the cat can communicate mind-to-mind with a human. The cat could, for example, receive the image of a gathering thunderstorm and then mentally project it to the witch. Many people know how to communicate to their animals, but witches know how to listen when their animals do the communicating.

The final and most powerful bond between witch and familiar, between human and cat, is just that—*love*. It is the feeling which transcends the barrier between one species and another on this planet. When this barrier is crossed, all kinds of psychic powers are doubled and more readily available. Both witch and cat know this. And if you and your cat love each other, you probably know this too.

CHAPTER 10

Phantasms

For thar's a thousand reasons that I won't take time to tell,
Why I am bound to b'lieve a cat is back and forth from hell.

From an old southern song.

Who purrs by the grave of unshriven dead,
while witches dance and ghouls are fed?

Joseph Payne Brennan, *The Cat!*, 1950.

Throughout history people have linked cats with things they don't understand. In earlier times cats were associated with deities. Later they were thought to be allied with devils. It's not surprising, then, that cats have also been connected with death and the beyond.

The Egyptians took great pains to prepare their deceased cats for the journey into the afterworld. They carried their cats long distances to cities, such as Bubastis and Sakkara, where the cats would be properly mummified and entombed. When times were bad in Egypt, such as during the Greco-Roman period beginning in 332 B.C., the Egyptians would travel to the cities to ask certain temple cats to speak to the gods on their behalf. The Egyptians would then donate the mummy of their cat to the cat who had interceded for them.

The association of cats with death has been common in other parts of the world as well. Natives on the Gold Coast of West Africa believed that when they died their soul would pass into the body of a cat. Some Japanese had a similar belief. They believed that a black spot on a cat was a sign that the cat's soul was that of one of their ancestors.

In China the souls of Buddhists were thought to reside in cats before passing on to paradise. Some Buddhists still believe that when a cat dies, its soul will speak of his owner to the Buddha.

There is also a legend that says that in Burma the Khmer people had a temple to the goddess Lao-Tsun, which contained 100 pure white cats. One cat, named Sinh, was the companion of Mun-Ha, an old priest. One night, as Mun-Ha was kneeling before the goddess, the temple was attacked by Thai raiders who murdered him on the spot. Sinh immediately jumped upon Mun-Ha's body and turned toward the goddess. The soul of the priest entered the cat, and the cat became a golden color with bright blue eyes so that it resembled the goddess. Its legs turned brown but its feet, where they touched the priest, remained pure white. The other priests saw this and were inspired to drive off the attackers. Seven days later, Sinh died taking Mun-Ha's soul to paradise. The following morning all the cats looked like Sinh. The priests believed the cats had taken possession of the souls of priests; they closely guarded the cats from that point on. These cats became the breed called the Birman.

When a monarch died in Siam (now Thailand), a cat would be entombed with him. A system of holes was built into the tomb so that the cat could get out. The cat's emergence from the tomb signified that the soul of the deceased had escaped to the afterworld. The cat was then captured and carried with great pomp and circumstance to the temple.

The link between cats and death has not always been positive. People have long believed that, if given the chance, a cat will suck away the breath of a baby. It was also believed that, if a cat was allowed near a corpse, it would steal the soul and the deceased would become a vampire. A vampire cat with two tails appears in Japanese folktales, as does an old sorcerer, who turns himself into a cat and enters people's houses to eat disobedient children.

Cats Are Queer Articles

This version of the old British tale, *The King of the Cats*, was told by Mr. Buckley, a tailor in Cork, Ireland, to Eric Cross in 1942.

I tell you, cats are the queer articles. You never know where you are with them. They seem to be different to every other class of animals. In the old days there were some foreign peoples who worshipped them, and it is not to be greatly wondered at, when you think of the intelligence of cats.

I had a strange thing happened to myself years ago with cats. It was many, many years ago now. I had a calf to sell, and it was the time of the November fair in Macroom. I'd borrowed the loan of a crib and horse from a neighbor, and was ready to set off for the fair about one o'clock in the morning.

Well, it came to one o'clock and I got up. I opened the door, and the night was so black that you would scarcely know which foot you were putting before you. I stirred up the fire and put some sticks under the kettle to make a cup of tea, and while it was boiling I went out to tackle up the horse. There was a mist coming down, so that I was wet enough already by the time that I had that job done.

I made the tea, and while I was drinking it I thought what a foolish thing it was for me to be getting out of a warm bed and going into the cold, wet night and traveling for twenty-four miles through the night. But it had to be done, so I buttoned up a grand frieze coat I had, and off we set. The horse was as unwilling as myself for the road, and the two of us were ashamed to look each other in the face, knowing the class of fools we were. We traveled for hours and hours, and not much of the first hour had gone before I was wet through and through.

As we drew nearer to the town I could see the lights in the farms by the roadside, where the people were getting up for the fair who had not to lose a night's sleep to get there. There was a regular

A cat in an Irish home, 1800s.

procession now on the road of calves and cattle being driven into the fair, but it was still dark and the daylight was only just coming.

Well, I took my place in the fair, and no one came to me and made me an offer for a long time. I thought that things were not going too well with me. Then a few asked me, but were offering only a poor price. I saw other cattle being driven away, and men I knew told me to sell, for it was a bad fair and prices were low. So at last I did sell, for the heart had gone out of me with the loss of sleep, and the long journey and the cold and the long waiting.

I tell you that I was a miserable man, standing there with ne'er a bite to eat and wet to the skin, and with the prospect of the long journey home again, and the poor pay I had for my suffering. When I got the money I had something to eat and made a few purchases, and then I thought that if any man ever earned a drink it was me. So I met some friends and we had a few drinks together, and then parted and went our different ways.

I let the horse go on at her own pace, with the reins hanging loose. The rain came down again, and the power of the drink soon wore off, and I wrapped myself up in my misery. With the sound and the swing of the crib and the creaking of the wheels and the darkness coming down again I fell asleep, as many a man does on the long way home from a winter's fair.

Now and again someone passed me on the road, but I scarcely heard them at all. For miles and miles I went; now asleep, now awake, with all manner of queer notions running in my head, as does happen to a man when he is exhausted.

As I was passing the graveyard of Inchigeela a cat put his head through the railings and said to me, "Tell Balgeary that Balgury is dead." I paid little heed to that, for my head was full of strange notions. I continued on my way. At last I reached home again, and untackled the horse and watered it and fed it, and then went into the house to change out of my wet clothes.

Herself started on me straightaway. 'Tis wonderful the energy that does be in a woman's tongue and the blindness that can be in her eyes, for I was in no mood for talk.

"Well," she said, "what sort of a fair was it?"

"Ah! the same as all fairs," said I.

"Did you get a good price?"

"I did not," said I.

"Were there many at the fair?" she asked then.

"The usual number, I suppose. Did you expect me to count them?"

"Did ye hear any news while you were in the town?"

There was no end to her questions.

"Hold your tongue," I said, "and give me the tea."

I drank the tea and had a bite to eat and began to feel better. Still she kept on asking me questions.

"Glory me! Fancy going in all that way and hearing nothing at all," she said, when I had no news for her. "You might as well have

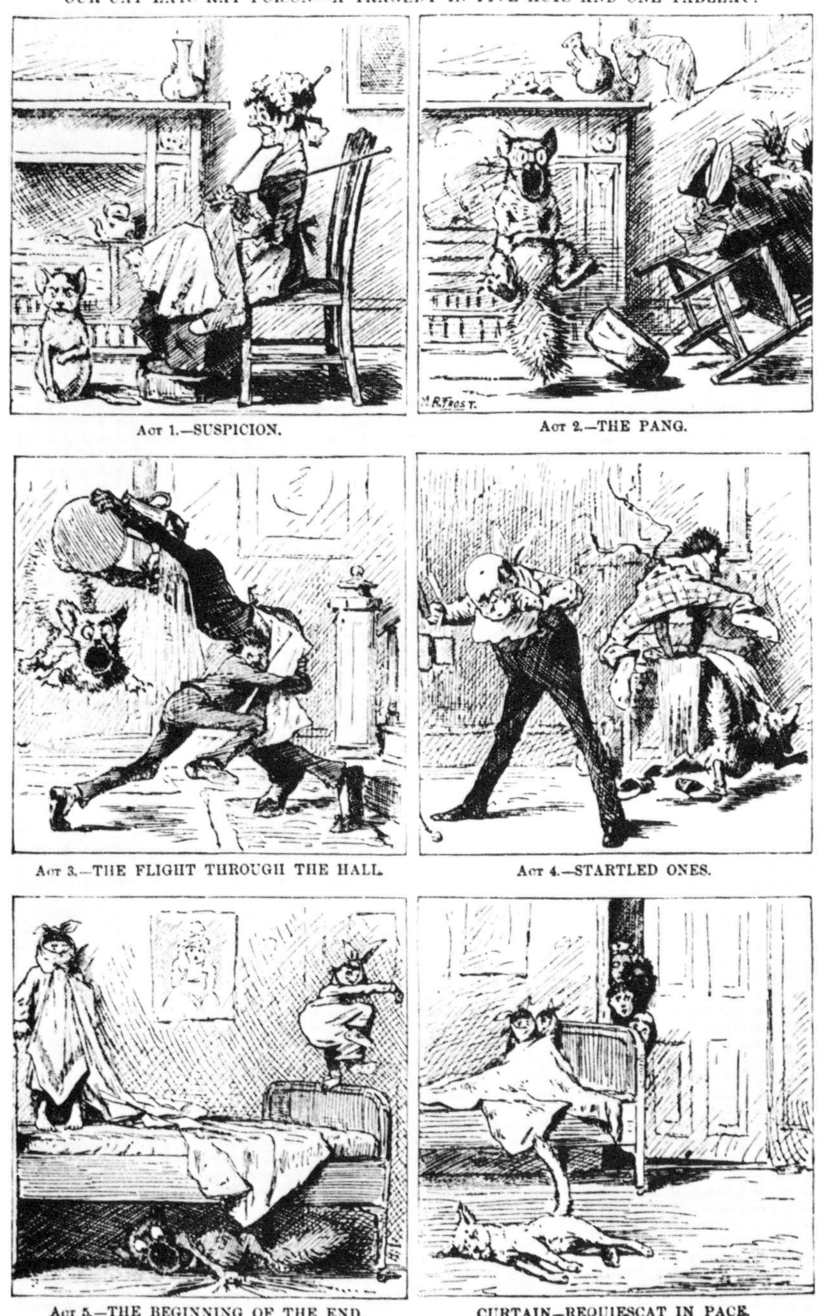

Our Cat Eats Rat Poison, A. B. Frost, *Harper's Magazine*, July 1881.

stayed at home for all the good that you get out of a fair."

I got up from the table and sat by the fire and lit my pipe, but still she plagued me and pestered me with her questions. Had I seen this one? Was I speaking with that one? Was there any news of the other one?

I suppose that the tea and the fire and the tobacco softened me. News and gossip are almost life to a woman, and she bore the hardness of our life as well, and I had brought her nothing home. Then I remembered the cat.

"The only thing that happened to me today," I said, "that has not happened on all fair days, was that when I was passing the graveyard of Inchigeela a cat stuck his head out of the railings."

"Wisha! there is nothing strange in that," she took me up.

"As I passed it called up to me, 'Tell Balgeary that Balgury is dead.' "

At that, the cat, sitting before the fire, whipped round on me. "The Devil fire you!" said he, "why didn't you tell me before? I'll be late for the funeral." And with that and no more, he leapt over the half-door, and was gone like the wind, and from that day to this we have seen no sign of him.

George Cruikshank (1792–1878).

Wait till Martin Comes

An old southern tale recorded by W. E. Chilton, Jr., of Charleston, West Virginia, on April 16, 1925.

Speakin' ob hants, Uncle were comin' home fum ch'ch one night w'en de clouds begin ter gather. Uncle had on his seersucker suit an' he know dat if de rain fall on it it were gwine ter tighten up on him. So he drapped in an ol' house by de roadside, which wuz said wuz hanted. Uncle he didn' pay no min' ter hants; he wuz a good man an' he had de Bible wid 'im. So he built hisself a fiah, an' stahted in ter read de book. Pretty soom de rain it gin ter fall.

Uncle he bin readin' in de Bible 'bout five minutes, w'en in walked a cat w'at's blacker'n a coal. Dis cat walk ober ter de fiahplace an' sot down in it. Den he picked up her chunck ob libe coal an' licked it, jis' like dat he licked it. Uncle he don' pay no min'; he's got cats of his own at home an' he knows all 'bout 'em. He read on in de book.

In 'bout two minutes, in walk anudder cat w'at's bigger'n a bulldog an' blacker'n de fus' one. He sot down in de fiah an' pick up a libe coal like dis an' dus' his cheeks wid it, dus' his cheeks wid it, he did. Den he tu'n ter de fus' cat an' say, "Is we ready?" An' de fus' cat he say, "Us better wait till Martin comes." Uncle he jump all de way f'um Exodus ter Isaiah, he's readin' so fas'. He ain't never heerd no cats talk befo', an' it worry 'im.

In 'bout two minutes mo', in comes a cat w'at's blacker'n de udder two an' bigger'n a wolf. He walk ober an' sot down in de fiah wid de udder cats an' he picked up a libe coal an' he dus' his eyeballs wid it, he dus' his eyeballs wid it, he do. Den he tu'n to de fus' cat w'at been doin all de talkin' an' he say, "Shall we do it now?" An' de fus' cat he say, "Us better wait till Martin comes."

Uncle close de book. As he went out der winder he say, "Goodnight, cats. W'en Martin comes, you tell 'im I *were* here."

Racing with a Black Cat

HOWARD W. ODUM, from *Cold Blue Moon, Black Ulysses Afar Off*, 1931. American writer.

Well, I heard 'bout black-cat ghost myself. One time fellow wus road hustlin' down that lonesome road. So when night ketches him he seen house. So he asks man to let him stay all night. "No," he says, "I got mo' chillun than I can bed, but there's house up 'bout mile nobody can stay in."

So he asks him why, an' he says it's ha'nted. "That ain't nothin'," fellow tells him, "I ain't skeered o' no ha'nts."

So he goes up 'bout dark, gits a lot o' light'ood an' wood, and built him big fire, roasted some 'taters, got box to set on, an' sholy

Richelieu's Cats, Peter DeSeve.

was feelin' lucky, 'cause started rainin' 'bout that time. So he dozed off to sleep. Long 'bout twelve o'clock wus woke up by sound, so he gits up lookin' fer ghost; got light'ood stick an' looks all through house. Eve'ything wus quiet an' wus nothin' he could see, so he says, "Well, this is fine." So thought he would pile down on flo' in front of fire an' go to sleep. So down he sot to pull off his old shoes. So he sot there bakin' his feet an' must a' nodded off 'cause all of sudden he felt wus company in room. So he looked an' door wus shet, window wus shet, but still he look 'roun' and turr'blest thing he ever seen. Thing looked at him, he looked at thing, settin' right on end of box. Sholy wus settin' up, jes' bones, no skin, jes' bones, knees stickin' out an' techin' his leg. Oh, Lawd, creepin' feelin' all over fellow; wus shakin' so till thing jes' rattled self again an' grin at him.

So all of sudden this ghost turned into big black cat. 'Bout that time it ups an' says, "Seem like ain't no body here but me an' you to-night." So this fellow says, "If I can jes' stand up little bit, won't be nobody here but you." So fellow gives mighty holler an' left through window an' run an' run, gettin' mo' skeerder ever' minute he run, till he jus' drop down in road. So big hollow voice meows at his elbow, "Sholy wus some race." Race, hell, that cat didn't know nuthin' 'bout race an' runnin'. Nex' time fellow didn't run, good God, he flew an' bu'st in man's house what sent him up to old house. So this man says, "Hell, you skeered me 'bout to death; but whut you got on yo' neck?" So fellow look an' had brung whole blamed winder-sash clean all way from other house. So man asks him if he wus going back after his shoes. Fellow tells him guess they can stay up there wid 'bout one hundred mo' pairs he seen settin' by fire.

A Roman floor mosaic found at Orange, France.

Chu Ling, ca. 1800s. Chinese artist.

(Untitled)

An old verse of unknown origin.

Black cat, black cat—when he cross yo' track
No matter whar you gwine,
To a dippin' or a dyin'
No matter whar you hurryin'
To a marrying or a buryin'
    You better turn back.

De Black Cat Crossed His Luck

JAMES DAVID CORROTHERS, from *The Black Cat Club*, 1902. American writer.

Den to de canjah-man Sam sped,
An' dis am whut de canjah-man said:
"Black Cat am a pow'ful man;
Ruinin' mor'tals am his plan.
Ole Satan an' de 'Riginal Sin
Am de daddy on' mammy o' him.
He's got nine hunderd an' ninety-nine libes—
Nineteen thousan' an' ninety-nine wibes—
He's kin to cholera an' allied
To smallpox on de mammy's side.
An' all de ebils on de earf
Stahted at de Black Cat's birf!—
Jes' stop an' die right whah you's at,
Ef yo' luck bin crossed by de ole Black Cat!"

An' den Sam read in history
Dat a cat crossed Pharaoh by de see,
An' burried him, as sho's you bo'n,
Too deep to heah ole Gabriel's ho'n!
An' dat de cat crossed Jonah once,
An' made him ack a regular dunce.
Crossed Bonaparte at Waterloo,
An' got Jeems Blaine defeated too.
"Oh, Laud a-mussy now on me!"
Cried Sam, "an' on dis history!"
An' den Sam went an' killed de cat—
Swo'e he'd make an end o' dat;—
Burried him in de light o' de moon,
Wid a rabbit's foot an' a silver spoon.
But de Black Cat riz, an' swallered him whole—
Bu'nt his house an' took his soul!

The Black Cat, 16th-century woodcut.

L'Evangile du Diable

(The Devil's Bible—excerpt)

Only imbiciles do not know that all cats have a pact with the Devil. . . . You can understand why cats sleep or pretend to sleep all day long, beside the fire in winter or in the sun in the summer. It is their task to patrol the barns and stables all night, to see everything, to hear everything. And you can deduce from that why the Evil Spirits, warned just in time, always manage to vanish away, to disappear before we can see them.

(Untitled)

An old Irish saying.

There's crocks of gold in all the forths [burial mounds], but there's cats and things guarding them.

A Strange Cat-Bat, R. P. Athanase Kircher, 1667.

CHAPTER 11

Life Beyond Time

Ah! cats are a mysterious kind of folk. There is more passing in their minds than we are aware of. It comes no doubt from their being so familiar with warlocks and witches.

Sir Walter Scott (1771–1832) to
Washington Irving.

The cat has a nervous ear, that turns this way and that.
And what the cat may hear, is known but to the cat.

David Morton (1886–1957).

Thus far we have looked at the cat from the point of view of humans; that is, how cats interact with our lives. In this chapter our focus shifts to the life of a cat. Obviously, the human perspective is difficult to move away from. Still, we can attempt to view the life of the cat through the mist of our human observation and interpretation.

As we have seen, what goes on in people's minds has played a large role in the lives of cats. The religious beliefs that people have may mean either a life of luxury for a cat or a life of persecution and painful death. These beliefs can also bring cats close to extinction, as happened in the Middle Ages, when cats were burned, along with witches.

It is interesting to note that, even during the height of the Roman Catholic church's persecution of cats, not one cat seems to have been excommunicated. From the 9th to the 20th centuries the church excommunicated almost every type of animal. In 1225 eels were booted out of the church. In 1386 at Falaise, France, a sow was expelled, and in 1389 at Dijon a horse was ostracized. An ox was banished in 1405. Rats and bloodsuckers were ousted at Bern, Switzerland, in 1451. In Delémont in 1906 a Swiss dog was one of the last animals to be excommunicated. Somehow cats seemed to have avoided this disgrace, an odd circumstance given the church's belief that all cats were in cahoots with Satan.

Cats didn't escape the long arm of the law during this period, though. Not only were they sentenced to death in witch trials, but they also appeared in non-occult-related litigations. In fact, all kinds of animals were involved in legal proceedings as plaintiff, defendant, or even as witness. At one trial in France during the 1500s, it is said that a defense attorney pleaded that his clients, some rats, couldn't appear in court because they were afraid to pass through the cat territory that lay between them and the court. This argument satisfied the court and the rats were acquitted of the charges against them.

Although society has advanced considerably since the Middle Ages, cats are still the subjects of atrocities. In the Far East there are countries where cats are eaten. In the West pet cats are picked up off the street and used to train pit bulls or made into imitation mink coats, gloves, and teddy bears.

Setting these injustices aside, what is the life of the average cat like? How intelligent are cats? Do they know things that we don't know? In the 15th century, people believed that only humans had intelligence. Descartes (1596–1650), one of the leading influences on Western thought, said that all animals are automatons, unfeeling objects whose sole existence is for the utilization and pleasure of people. Thus humans could treat animals in any manner they saw fit, for there was no need to treat them humanely. This line of reasoning prompted Ambrose Bierce in 1911 to come up with the definition, "Cat, n. A soft, indestructible automaton provided by nature to be kicked when things go wrong in the domestic circle."

Although many people still cling to these ideas, today's scientists are proving that they are wrong. Researcher Francine Patterson has succeeded in teaching a gorilla, Koko, to talk using sign language. Some people, such as neurophysiologist John Lilly, believe that whales and dolphins may be more intelligent than we are.

So what about cats: Could they be smarter than we suspect?

Cat's Company, F. Bellew, 19th century.

(Untitled)

The Conjurors' Magazine, 1791.

In the new moon gather the herb nepe, and dry it in the heat of the sun, when it is temperately hot: gather vervain in the hour of Mercury, and only expose it to the air while the Sun is under the earth. Hang these together in a net, in a convenient place, and when a cat has scented it, her cry will soon call those about her that are within hearing; and they will rant and run about, leaping and capering to get at the net, which must be hung or placed so that they cannot easily accomplish it, for they will nearly tear it to pieces. Near Bristol there is a field that goes by the appellation of the '*Field of Cats*,' from a large number of these animals being drawn together there by this contrivance.

Instinct vs. Reason—A Black Cat

EDGAR ALLEN POE (1809–1849). American poet and short-story writer.

The line which demarcates the instinct of the brute creation from the boasted reason of man, is, beyond doubt, of the most shadowy and unsatisfactory character—a boundary line far more difficult to settle than even the North-Eastern or the Oregon. The question whether the lower animals do or do not reason, will possibly never be decided—certainly never in our present condition of knowledge. While the self-love and arrogance of man will persist in denying the reflective power to beasts, because the granting it seems to derogate from his own vaunted supremacy, yet he perpetually finds himself involved in the paradox of decrying instinct as an inferior faculty, while he is forced to admit its infinite superiority, in a thousand cases, over the very reason which he claims exclusively as his own. Instinct, so far from being an inferior reason, is perhaps the most exacted intellect of all. It will appear to the true philosopher as the divine mind itself acting *immediately* upon its creatures.

The habits of the lion-ant, of many kinds of spiders, and of the beaver, have in them a wonderful analogy, or rather similarity, to the usual operations of the reason of man—but instinct of some other creatures has no such analogy—and is referable only to the spirit of the Deity itself, acting *directly*, and through no corporal organ, upon the volition of the animal. Of this lofty species of instinct the coral-worm affords a remarkable instance. This little creature, the architect of precision of purpose, and scientific adaptation and arrangement, from which the most skillful engineer might imbibe his best knowledge—but is gifted with what humanity does not possess—with the absolute spirit of prophecy. It will foresee, for months in advance, the pure accidents which are to happen in its dwelling, and aided by myriads of its brethren, all acting as if with one mind (and *indeed* acting with only one—with the mind of the Creator) will work diligently to counteract influences which exist alone in the future. There is also an immensely wonderful consideration connected with the cell of the bee. Let a mathematician be required to solve the problem of the shape best calculated in such a cell as the bee wants, for the two requisites of strength and space—and he will find himself involved in the very highest and most abstruse questions of analytical research. Let him be required to tell the number of sides which will give to the cell the greatest space, with the greatest solidity, and to define the exact angle at which, with the same object in view, the roof must incline—and to answer the query, he must be a Newton or a Laplace. Yet since bees were, they have been continually solving the problem. The leading distinction and reason seems to be, that, while the one is infinitely the more exact, the more certain, and the more far-seeing in its sphere of action—the sphere of action in the other is of the far wider extent. But we are preaching a homily, when we merely intended to tell a short story about a cat.

The writer of this article is the owner of one of the most remarkable black cats in the world—and this is saying much; for it will be remembered that black cats are all of them witches. The one in question has not a white hair about her, and is of a demure and sanctified demeanor. That portion of the kitchen which she most frequents is accessible only by a door, which closes with what is termed a thumblatch; these latches are rude in construction, and some force and dexterity are always necessary to force them down. But puss is in the daily habit of opening the door, which she accomplishes in the following way. She first springs from the ground to the guard of the latch (which resembles the guard over a gun-trigger), and through this she thrusts her left arm to hold on with. She now, with her right hand, presses the thumblatch until it yields, and here several attempts are frequently requisite. Having forced it down, however, she seems to be aware that her task is but half accomplished, since, if the door is not pushed open before she lets go, the latch will again fall into its socket. She, therefore,

Poe with his cat, Catalina, who perched on his shoulder when he wrote; Charles Smeldon, 19th century.

screws her body round so as to bring her hind feet immediately beneath the latch, while she leaps with all her strength from the door—the impetus of the spring forcing it open, and her hind feet sustaining the latch until this impetus is fairly given.

We have witnessed this singular feat a hundred times at least, and never without being impressed with the truth of the remark with which we commenced this article—that the boundary between instinct and reason is of a very shadowy nature. The black cat, in doing what she did, must have made use of all the perceptive and reflective faculties which we are in the habit of supposing the prescriptive qualities of reason alone.

There is Always Another, Marcus Stone (1840–1921). English painter.

Siva and Vishnu

MELANIE SCHNEIDER, from *Cat People*, 1978. Television and radio producer.

They can open all of the doors, drawers, and closets in the house. I will be sitting in the living room with company and suddenly underwear—socks, bras, panties, everything—will just arrive in the living room. I also have to hide the telephone under the sofa if I'm not around. They will answer the phone and leave it off the hook. When I am eating at the table, the cats will go into the kitchen cabinet and bring me the entire box of napkins.

They are much more fun in twos.

William Morris Hunt (1824–1879).

The Fireside Sphinx (excerpt)

AGNES REPPLIER, 1901. American essayist.

A female cat is kept young in spirit and supple in body by the restless vivacity of her kittens. She plays with her little ones, fondles them, pursues them if they roam too far, and corrects them sharply for all the faults to which feline infancy is heir. A kitten dislikes being washed quite as much as a child does, especially in the neighbourhood of its ears. It tries to escape the infliction, rolls away, paddles with its little paws, and behaves as naughtily as it knows how, until a smart slap brings it suddenly back to subjection. Pussy has no confidence in moral suasion, but implicitly follows Solomon's somewhat neglected advice. I was once told a pleasant story of an English cat who had reared several large families, and who, dozing one day before the nursery fire, was disturbed and annoyed by the whining of a fretful child. She bore it as long as she could, waiting for the nurse to interpose her authority; then, finding passive endurance had outstripped the limits of her patience, she arose, crossed the room, jumped on the sofa, and twice with her strong soft paw, which had chastised many an erring kitten, deliberately boxed the little girl's ears,—after which she returned to her slumbers.

(Untitled)

FATHER HUE, 19th century. A missionary to China.

Our obliging converts brought us three or four cats and explained how one could use a cat as a watch. They showed us that the pupil of his eyes contracted steadily as mid-day approached, that at mid-day it was like a hair, like an extremely fine line drawn perpendicularly on the eye. After mid-day, the dilation began again. When we had carefully examined all the cats, we decided that it was past mid-day—all the eyes were in agreement.

(Untitled)

CHARLES BAUDELAIRE, from *Revue Fantaisiste*, 1861. French poet and critic.

One day, a missionary, walking in a Nanking suburb, noticed that he had forgotten his watch and asked a little boy the time.

The little boy hesitated at first, then, on reflection, replied "I will find out." Shortly after, he returned with a big cat in his arms,

Shen Shou, 1494, Ming Dynasty. Chinese artist.

and looking straight into its eyes, he said without hesitation "It's not quite mid-day yet." Which was correct.

When I take in my arms this extraordinary cat, at once the pride of his race, the joy of my heart and the perfume of my spirit, whether by night or day, in full sunlight or dark shadow, in the depths of his adorable eyes, I always distinctly read the hour, always the same, a vast, solemn hour big as space, without minutes or seconds, a motionless hour not marked on clocks, and yet light as a sigh, as a glance.

And if someone came to disturb me while I watched this lovely dial, if a dishonest and intolerant spirit came to say "What do you watch with such attention, what do you seek in the eyes of that creature? Do you see the time, idle and wasteful mortal?" I would reply without hesitating "Yes, I see the time, it is Eternity."

(Untitled)

ANONYMOUS, from *English Mechanic* magazine, 1892.

Mr. J. McNair Wright, an American naturalist, has called attention to a case of "fascination" by a cat which came under his observation. The cat was sitting on the sill of his window near a pine tree, when a bird alighted on a tree. The cat fixed his eyes on the bird with a peculiar intensity of expression, and the fur on his head stood on end, but otherwise he remained motionless. The bird quivered, trembled, looked fixedly at the cat, and, finally, with a feeble shake of the wings, fell towards the cat, who pounced upon it. Mr. Wright regards such fascination of snakes and other animals as a form of hypnotism.

The Cats

JAN STRUTHER (1901–1953), from *Punch* magazine. British novelist and poet.

In Sycamore Square
At the crack of dawn
The white cats play
On the grey green lawn;
One is the owner
Of Number Three
And the other pretends
To belong to me.
Slowly over
The dew-soaked grass
Their low tense bodies
Like serpents pass,
And each imperceptible
Smooth advance
Is an intricate step
In a mystic dance,
Which ends in the cat
From Number Three
Rushing quite suddenly
Up a tree.
While mine walks off with a dignified air
To the other end of Sycamore Square.
But nobody yet has ever found out
What in the world
The game's about.

The Cat and the Ball of Thread, Theophile Steinlen, (1859–1923), from *Des chats*. French writer and artist.

When the Wind and the Rain

ELIZABETH J. COATSWORTH, from *The Sparrow Bush*, 1966. American poet and writer.

Today the cats are wild:
they stand upright,
and with their claws unsheathed
rake cushioned chairs;
the sofa's polished legs
have felt their spite;
they chase each other headlong
down the stairs.

Go not on a long journey,
stay indoors.
The wind is rising
and the rains will come.
The cats have summoned them:
along the floors
a coldness flows,
and thunder beats his drum.

Go not afield,
for once, stay home with me.
The fire is on the hearth,
the house is warm;
and purring, nodding, drowsing
sleepily,
the cats sit, now
that they have raised the storm.

Edward Gorey, from *Amphigory Also*, 1983.

The Century Cat, James Carter Beard (1837–1913), from *Century* magazine. American illustrator and editor.

(Untitled)

REVEREND SAMUEL BISHOP (1731–1795). English schoolmaster and poet.

If with her tail puss played in frolic mood,
Herself pursuing, by herself pursued;
"See!" cried my nurse, "she bids for rain prepare,
A storm, be sure, is gathering in the air;
If near the fire the kitten's back was found,
Frost was at hand, and snows hung hovering round;
Her paw prophetic rais'd above her ear
Foretold a visit, for some friend was near.

Kittens, W. A. Rogers.

(Untitled)

ANDREW LANG (1844–1912). Scottish scholar, folklorist, and poet.

From the dawn of creation the cat has known his place, and he has kept it, practically untamed and unspoiled by man. He has *retenue*. Of all animals, he alone attains to the Contemplative Life. He regards the wheel of existence from without, like the Buddha. There is no pretense of sympathy about the cat. He lives alone, aloft, sublime, in a wise passiveness. . . .

Everyone is aware that a perfectly comfortable, well-fed cat will occasionally come to his house and settle there, deserting a family by whom it is lamented, and to whom it could, if it chose, find its way back with ease. This conduct is a mystery which may lead us to infer that cats form a great secret society, and that they come and go in pursuance of some policy connected with education, or perhaps with witchcraft.

Sea Cats at Dusk

BIANCA BRADBURY, from *Yankee* magazine. American poet.

At six o'clock the boats come in,
At six o'clock the cats come down—
The Harbor Street Irregulars,
The highwaymen who haunt the town
Report for duty. Weathered piers
Are crowned with furry ornament,
Heads high, tails furled. They stare and stare
And sniff for news of fish. They sent
Their blessings with the boats at dawn,
And now the wise but weary crews,
Grumbling at the blackmailers,
Toss out the tribute, pay their dues.

La raie (The Ray), Jean Chardin, 1728. French painter.

A Certain Wisdom

RUTH MUNCH, from *Cat Fancy* magazine. American poet.

You curl the silence of your sleep,
one velvet paw curved like a shell
scooping an intrinsic substance
to cover your eyes.

Studies of a Cat, Beatrix Potter, June 2, 1903. British writer and illustrator.

I watch you in your world
and I grow wise.

You are a golden flash
that singles itself in shadows.
You carve your domain
from fence to house
then gather the rooms about you
for your own.
Each of your days is a world.

You do not look back on yesterday
nor do you anticipate tomorrow.
You live the present intensified
in its own way,
and trust my every circling of your world.

Cat Making Up, Tomoo Inagaki.

For One Who Lives with Me

FRANCIS MAGUIRE, from *Cat Fancy* magazine. American poet.

I'll move like a lion,
like water, like music,
I'll crouch like the Sphinx,
sit like Buddha,

sleep in a compact
circle of gold,
still as the sun,
as radiant.

And you, my sister,
my teacher in fur,
will stare your approval
and call me brother.

The Cat

LYTTON STRACHEY (1880–1932). English biographer.

Dear creature by the fire a-purr,
Strange idol, eminently bland,
Miraculous puss! As o'er your fur
I trail a negligible hand

And gaze into your gazing eyes,
And wonder in a demi-dream
What mystery it is that lies
Behind those slits that glare and gleam,

Miss Peck, Franz von Lenback, ca. 1890.

An exquisite enchantment falls
About the portals of my sense;
Meandering through enormous halls
I breathe luxurious frankincense.

An ampler air, a warmer June
Enfold me, and my wondering eye
Salutes a more imperial moon
Throned in a more resplendent sky

Than ever knew this northern shore.
Oh, strange! For you are with me too,
And I, who am a cat once more,
Follow the woman that was you.

With tail erect and pompous march,
The proudest puss that ever trod,
Through many a grove, 'neath many an arch,
Impenetrable as a god,

Down many an alabaster flight
Of broad and cedar-shaded stairs,
While over us the elaborate night
Mysterious gleams and glares!

Fur Traders Descending the Missouri, George Caleb Bingham, ca. 1845. American painter.

Cat

GEORGE BARR, from *Cat Fancy* magazine. American poet.

downstairs one floor
colored like old brass
glides like water over the grass
to rub my leg.
Maine small town summer landscape
changes to dusk.
The cat steals off to try out,
just for size,
the cardboard boxes I've stored in the barn.
Comes back.

We sit like jugs
and watch an old man,
in dungarees and green work shirt,
steer up the street on the end of his pipe.
Nobody near, I say to the cat
in a voice louder than a whisper:
"I won't tell anybody that you can talk,"
and look to the bottoms of his green eyes
that do not tell
what he feels, sees, hears, sighs.

CHAPTER 12

Secrets Among Moonlit Stones

Cats are mysterious beings . . . symbols of evil, gods of the Pharoahs. You never know if they love you or if they condescend to occupy your house. This mystery is what makes them the most attractive beast.

Paul Moore, Episcopal Bishop of New York, 1978.

I've met many thinkers and many cats, but the wisdom of cats is infinitely superior.

Hippolyte Taine (1828–1893), French philosopher.

In our exploration of cats, we have moved through the various perceptions people have of the world of the cat: cats in our daily lives, cats in myths, cats as demons, cats as gods and goddesses. In this chapter we enter the mysterious world of the cat.

As we march through life with our blinders securely in place we can be oblivious to what's beyond the edge of our perceived world; with the exception of those rare instances when the blinders are knocked slightly askew and the unfamiliar peeks out and winks at us. So now we will attempt to look at the world through our cat's eyes.

Curiously, if we compare this chapter with the previous chapters, we would find that it most resembles the first chapter. And so we have come full circle. We have journeyed farther and farther out until we have ended up at our point of origin, though looking at it from a different angle. Although this may surprise us, it wouldn't have surprised Albert Einstein. In Einstein's universe there were no straight lines, only great circles. Einstein predicted that if we were to travel out into space in what we perceived as a straight line we would eventually end up where we started.

This cyclical nature of the world is mirrored in ancient symbols, such as the snake swallowing its own tail and the sleeping cat curled in a circle. This idea also appears in the Hindu belief in reincarnation, where life is seen as moving from birth to death and death to rebirth in one great circle of being. One ends up back at the beginning point, though, hopefully, a little wiser.

In this chapter, we see how poetic intuition can give a different perspective on the world of the cat. This may be the closest we will ever get to knowing what is really going on in the mind of our cat since in the end all we can do is speculate as to what it's like to be a cat. We can sit back, observe, and try to imagine what our cat's life is like. Perhaps this is what our cat is doing when she observes us. She may be trying to decipher our incomprehensible actions; trying to understand our strange motivations, worries, and desires. She may decide that we are demented in the way we carry out our frenzied and entangled lives. She might even derive some amusement from our antics.

Perhaps her view of our world is distorted by her world just as our understanding of her motivations may be warped by our own desires and wishes. We talk to our cat and attribute to her human emotions. We assume that she understands us and we are surprised, even offended, when she appears not to. She may continue to catch birds and leave them on our doorstep no matter how much we try to teach her that we don't want birds to be harmed.

Likewise, perhaps she assumes that we understand her, and is just as puzzled when we don't. She lays her prize catch on the doorstep as the ultimate expression of her affection for us and, in return, we screech at her like a crazed maniac.

Thus we have two completely different worlds that are intimately intertwined. There is much cats can learn from us, just as there is much that we can learn from them. But whether we can ever truly understand the world of the cat may never be known.

The Graham Children (detail), William Hogarth (1697–1764). English painter and engraver.

In Connecticut There Are Cats

BETTY LOWRY, from *Yankee* magazine, 1967. American poet.

In Connecticut there are cats
Sitting on white porches, prowling
Through dandelions, sleeping
On sunny window seats. Sturdy
Yankee cats in Connecticut
Are black or white or orange
Striped with short practical coats
Battle scarred in brief domestic wars.
Connecticut cats care little
For dogs or men as they wash
Their fine morning faces, eschew
Synthetic city food for country
Cream and watch the New England
Spring come up the road as easily
As a cat himself. Redbud, dogwood,
Apple blossom take precedent
For an hour and then move on.
Connecticut cats have seen Springs come
And go. Window seats endure.

The Poison Tree (excerpt)

BANKIM CHANDRA CHATTERJEE, 1884. Bengali novelist.

Damal Mani [a young woman] is sitting in her sleeping chamber at her ease, needle in hand, sewing at some canvas work, her hair all loose; no one about but Satish Babu [her small child], indulging in many noises. Satish Babu at first tried to snatch away his mother's wool; but finding it securely guarded, he gave his mind to sucking the head of a clay tiger. In the distance a cat with outstretched paws sits watching them both. Her disposition was grave: her face indicated much wisdom, and a heart devoid of fickleness. She evidently was thinking—"the condition of human creatures is frightful; their minds are ever given to sewing of canvas, playing with dolls, or some such silly employment; their thoughts are not turned to good works, such as providing suitable food for cats. What will become of them hereafter!" . . . Then, seeing no means by which the disposition of mankind could be improved, the cat, heaving a sigh, slowly departs.

Detail of engraving, 1616.

A Troubled Sleep

ERIC BARKER, from *Yankee* magazine. American poet.

My cats in their huddled sleep
(Two heaps of fur made one)
Twitch their ears and whimper—
Do they dream the same dream?

Something's upset them both!
What's leering through the dark
Wherein they're so entwined
They shudder through each other,

Two creatures so involved
(Cat sister and cat brother)
They can but share as one
What nightmare shakes the other?

Gottfried Mind (1768–1814). Swiss painter.

And yet I've watched them creep,
Each one intent, alone,
Drawn to a single focus,
So passionately its own

Objective that they'd spit
(Cat sister or cat brother)
On which one dared presume
To trespass near the other.

I think the latter scene
(The unit not the plus)
Becomes both him and her
More than this unquiet fur

Of cats anonymous—
Even though they stalk a bird
That holds my breath to pray
It safely flies away—
I like them better thus.

Cat on the Porch at Dusk

DOROTHY HARRIMAN, from *The Christian Science Monitor*, 1952. American poet.

Near the edge, as on a shelf,
The patient cat combines himself.
Motionless he huddles there
Before the changing light, and broods
On daylight's deep ineptitudes.

When gradually the night takes place
He rises, stretching whiskers, toes
And stepping royally, he goes . . .
Slowly the darkness slides apart
And soundless, lets him in.

By Louis Wain (1860–1939), British artist, who was obsessed with cats. He eventually went insane and spent the last 15 years of his life in mental asylums. These pictures correspond with his losing touch with reality.

Unknown 19th-century artist.

The Cat

ANN STANFORD, from *Cat Fancy* magazine. American poet.

The cat by magic comes
Through slits of doors or air
To shadow through the rooms
And stalk what is not there.

And thrust outside by night,
With old and formal shout
In frightful guise she fights
The demons all about.

Then soft in sunny days,
Lulled in the leaves she goes.
No face of fiend dismays
Her vulnerable repose.

High on a Ridge of Tiles

MAURICE JAMES CRAIG (born 1919).

High on a ridge of tiles
A cat, erect and lean,
Looks down and slyly smiles;
The pointed ears are keen,
Listening for a sound
To rise from the backyard.
He casts upon the ground
A moment's cold regard.

Whatever has occurred
Is on so small a scale
That we can but infer
From the trembling of the tail
And the look of blank surprise
That glares out of the eyes
That underneath black fur
His face is deathly pale.

By Everett Shinn.

The Poet's Cat, Stephen Gooden, 1945.

Uncanny

ELLIOT WALKER, from *Cat Tales in Verse*, 1900.

There is something so peculiar in a cat's mysterious ways,
That I'm inclined to think I hit the mark
In hinting at affinities with beings we can't praise,
And do not like to think of after dark.

Have you noted, a cosy winter evening, in your chair,
You would start up with a sudden, "Oh, dear me!"
As you caught, intently gazing at a thing that wasn't there,
The feline member of your family?

Have you noticed how she listens with a sharp and anxious ear?
And how she moves her head along the wall?
And you get so very nervous at the things you cannot hear,
That you hardly dare to go to bed at all.

It is only that her senses, preternaturally keen,
At night are very, very wide-awake;
And she looks at trifling shadows on the ceiling or the screen,
That our dull, human vision does not take.

For the very softest footfall of a mouse in distant wall,
Does not escape that most attentive ear,
Which is tuned to fine accordance far beyond our human call.
Yet it sometimes make us feel a little queer.

I wish they wouldn't do so, for it isn't very nice
To have attention drawn from pleasant book,
And nervously imagine—when they only think of mice—
And feel a strange sensation, when they *look*.

Cat from the Night

HORTENSE ROBERTA ROBERTS, from *Kaleidograph Magazine*, 1951. American writer.

All night a branch of the cypress tree
Knocked on the pane till I broke it free
To thump to the ground. In a moment a scratch
Harried the door. I lifted the latch,
And a cat rushed in like death's dark wind.
He was blacker than crow-wings; his middle was thinned
To fear and hunger. Everywhere
I stepped he stepped, with his green-lit stare
And his pleading purr, till I fed him cream
While the wind in the tree was a witch-wailed scream.

Nights now, curled snug in the hearth fire's bliss
At a sound outside he will rise and hiss
With his back thrust high and his fur thrust higher
As he glares at the window with midnight ire.
And often by day in his windowed niche
His body will quiver, his tail will twitch,
As he stares at the bent, scarred cypress tree
And nothing else—that I can see.

Robert Seymour (ca. 1800–1836), from Shakespeare's *King Lear*. British illustrator and caricaturist. He illustrated many of Charles Dickens's novels.

Puck, Louis Wain (1860–1939). British artist.

Hearth

PEGGY BACON, from *Animosities*, 1931. American artist and writer.

A cat sat quaintly by the fire
   And watched the burning coals
And watched the little flames aspire
   Like small decrepit souls.
Queer little fire with coals so fat
   And crooked flames that rise,
No queerer than the little cat
   With fire in its eyes.

Nodding

STEVIE SMITH (1902–1971). British writer and illustrator.

Tisdal my beautiful cat
Lies on the old rag mat
In front of the kitchen fire.
Outside the night is black.

The great fat cat
Lies with his paws under him
His whiskers twitch in a dream.
He is slumbering.

The clock on the mantlepiece
Ticks unevenly, tic-toc, tic-toc
Good heavens what is the matter
With the kitchen clock?

Outside an owl hunts,
Hee hee hee hee,
Hunting in the Old Park
From his snowy tree.
What on earth can he find in the park tonight,
It is so wintry?

Now the fire burns suddenly too hot
Tizdal gets up to move,
Why should such an animal
Provoke our love?

The twigs from the elder bush
Are tapping on the window pane
As the wind sets them tapping,
Now the tapping begins again.

R. B. Birch (1849–1924), from *Little Lord Fauntleroy*.

One laughs on a night like this
In a room half firelight half dark
With a great lump of a cat
Moving on the hearth,
And the twigs tapping quick,
And the owl in an absolute fit.
One laughs supposing creation
Pays for its long plodding
Simply by coming to this—
Cat, night, fire—and a girl nodding.

R. B. Birch (1849–1924).

Companionship at Night

AGNES STEWART BECK, 1939. American poet.

An owl's weird cry comes across the hill
And I am alone tonight;
My mind conjures a dark ravine
With lifeless trees whose limbs
Outstretch as dying men's gaunt arms
Against a troubled sky,
Imploring mercy from a heedless God.

Draw close and purr, old yellow cat,
Though they call you a beast of prey,
But, oh, you're a living, breathing thing;
Warm blood flows through your veins,
And a little heart throbs beneath soft fur.
Draw close, old yellow cat,
For I am all alone—and cold—
And the owl's weird cry
Keeps coming across the hill all night.

Cat Alert, from Frank Leslie's *Christmas Box* magazine, 1857.

Black Cat

RAINER MARIA RILKE, from *New Poems*, 1908. German poet.

Glances even at an apparition
still seem somehow to reverberate;
here on this black fell, though, the emission
of your strongest gaze will dissipate:

as a maniac, precipitated
into the surrounding black, will be
halted headlong and evaporated
by his padded cell's absorbency.

All the glances she was ever swept with
on herself she seems to be concealing
where, with lowering and peevish mind they're
being downlooked upon her and slept with.
As if wakened, though, she turns her face
full upon your own quite suddenly,
and in the yellow amber of those sealing
eyes of hers you unexpectedly
meet the glance you've given her, enshrined there
like an insect of some vanished race.

Waiting for *It*

MAY SWENSON, from *To Mix with Time*, 1957. American poet.

My cat jumps to the window sill
and sits there still as a jug.
He's waiting for me, but I cannot be
coming, for I am in the room.

His snout, a gloomy V of patience,
pokes out into the sun.
The funnels of his ears expect
to be poured full of my footsteps.

It, the electric moment, a sweet
mouse, will appear; at his gray
eye's edge I'll be coming home
if he sits on the window ledge.

It is here, I say, and call him
to my lap. Not a hair
in the gap of his ear moves.
His clay gaze stays steady.

That solemn snout says: *It*
is what is about to happen, not
what is already here.

From the comic strip "Little Nemo in Slumberland," September 9, 1906, Windsor McCay. American cartoonist.

Deadly Nightshade, early 19th-century wood engraving.

Ah How My Cat Benjamin

PAULINE M. LEET, from *Harper's Magazine*, 1957. American poet.

Ah how my cat Benjamin flies this midnight
At the window glass, and droops his yellow length along the sill,
Moaning for the cat-cobbled streets and slit-lit lamps
Of his long half grown dreams. All shadows move
Beyond the glass, and mysteries of noise and smells unravel
Before dun sooted bodies hot hearted stalking still.

How I do desire in my glass room heavy at his shoulder
To unglass us both, were not my powers less than his
And spin us darkly tumbling to reproach the dogs
Amid stretching streets; and light green slant-eyed candles
In every darkened door and lair to enmity or love,
Till in a biding patient day, we lick real wounds in an open place.

On a Night of Snow

ELIZABETH J. COATSWORTH. American poet and writer.

Cat, if you go out-doors you must walk in the snow.
You will come back with little white shoes on your feet,
Little white slippers of snow that have heels of sleet.
Stay by the fire, my cat. Lie still, do not go.
See how the flames are leaping and hissing low,
I will bring you a saucer of milk like a marguerite,
So white and so smooth, so spherical, and so sweet—
Stay with me, Cat. Out-doors the wild winds blow.

Out-doors the wild winds blow, Mistress, and dark is the night.
Strange voices cry in the trees, intoning strange lore,
And more than cats move, lit by our eyes' green light,
On silent feet where the meadow grasses hang hoar—
Mistress, there are portents abroad of magic and might,
And things that are yet to be done. Open the door!

Angora Cat, Morris Hirshfield, 1937–39.

One O'clock

KATHERINE PYLE, from *The Wonder Clock*, 1887. American poet.

One of the Clock, and silence deep
Then up the Stairway, black and steep
The old House-Cat comes creepy-creep
With soft feet goes from room to room
Her green eyes shining through the gloom,
    And finds all fast asleep.

Unknown Japanese artist.

The Cat

WILLIAM HENRY DAVIES (1871–1940). British tramp and poet.

Within that porch, across the way,
I see two naked eyes this night;
Two eyes that neither shut nor blink,
Searching my face with a green light.

But cats to me are strange, so strange—
I cannot sleep if one is near;
And though I'm sure I see those eyes,
I'm not so sure a body's there!

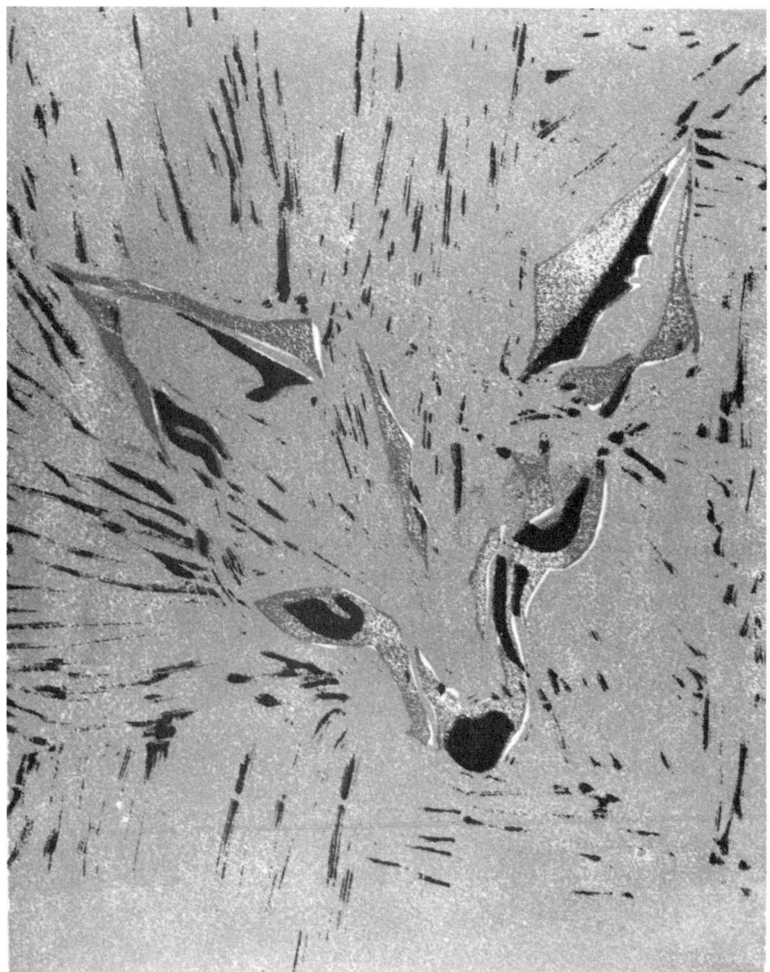

Rose, Mary Beth DiVito, 1987.

Unknown artist, 1700s.

Villanelle for the Cat

PHILIP DACEY, from *Cat Fancy* magazine, 1972. American poet and professor.

My supple ways are deep as water's ways.
The moves I make embody what I know.
I lift my paw and make a secret sign.

I have a history of blood and grace.
I honor it by pacing to and fro.
My subtle ways are deep as water's ways.

I move in keeping with a god's design.
I'm moving quickest when I'm moving slow.
I lift my paw and make a secret sign,

My body translates mysteries with ease.
My body is the Book of How to Go.
I swear my ways are deep as water's ways.

I send a message with my arching spine
But keep back more a message than I show.
I lift my paw and give a secret sign.

By feinting at a ghost I offer praise.
I recognize what's high by crouching low.
My supple ways are deep as water's ways.
I lift my paw and trace a secret sign.

The Cats of Pfeffa-Rah

JOHN RICHARD STEPHENS, 1988.

Late at night when we're asleep
And black shadows start to creep
    Cats begin to stir and heed the call.
Off they drift into the night
Guided by their second sight
    To perform a secret ritual.

Through the woods and decayed leaves
Where the netherworld unweaves
    Silent cats approach from all around.
As effervescent vapours glide
And the spastic weasels hide
    Wolves, in fear, do quiver at every sound.

Gathered at a sacred site
To conduct their ancient rite
    Wraiths, like violent winds, around them swirl.
Casting spells in an attack
Trying to bring their gods back
    So that Pfeffa-Rah can rule the world.

Out across the moonlit plain
Come the screams of dogs insane
    As the cat's dark power begins to grow.
Lightning blasts down from the sky.
Earthquakes echo in reply.
    Something stirs in decayed tombs below.

But too soon there comes the dawn
And, for now, their chance is gone.
    It was only one of many tries.
As we wake up from our sleep
Our cat is purring at our feet
    Looking up at us with loving eyes.

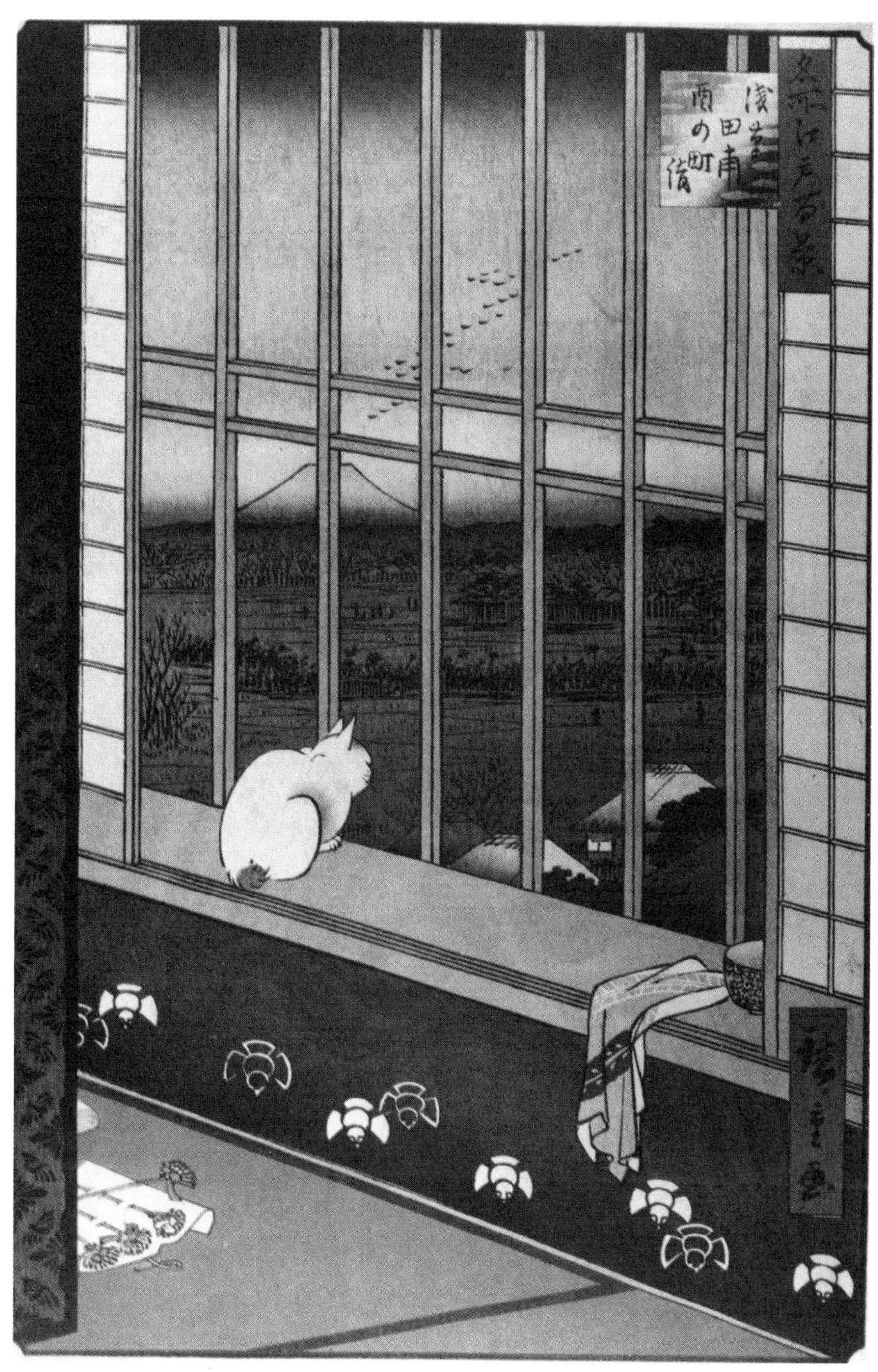

Akakusa tanbo Torinomachi mode (Akakusa Ricefields and Torinomachi Festival), Ando Hiroshige, from *One Hundred Famous Views of Edo*, 1857.

Credits

My thanks to the following, who have granted permission to reprint copyrighted material. Every effort has been made to reach owners of copyrighted material. I apologize for any inadvertant omissions and will be grateful if such are brought to my attention.

Frontispiece: Untitled drawing by Robert Ingpen. Copyright © 1985 by Robert Ingpen. Reprinted by permission of the artist.

Page 3: "Cat in the Rain" by Ernest Hemingway. Reprinted with permission of Charles Scribner's Sons, an imprint of Macmillan Publishing Company from *In Our Time* by Ernest Hemingway. Copyright 1925 by Charles Scribner's Sons; copyright renewed 1953 by Ernest Hemingway.

Page 10: Untitled story by Apion as quoted by Michel Eyquem de Montaigne. From *Great Books of the Western World*, Vol. 25, Robert Maynard Hutchins, ed. Reprinted with permission from Encyclopedia Britannica, Inc.

Page 15: "Rendezvous" from *Honorable Cat,* by Paul Gallico. Copyright © 1972 by Paul Gallico and Mathemata Anstalt. Reprinted by Permission of Crown Publisher, a Division of Random House Inc.

Page 19: "Bravo" by Philip Dacey. Copyright © 1989 by Philip Dacey. Reprinted by permission of the author.

Page 26: "The Kitten," from *Verses from 1929 On* by Ogden Nash. Copyright © 1940 by Ogden Nash. Reprinted by permission of Little, Brown and Company and Curtis Brown, Ltd.

Page 35: "The Bad Kittens" by Elizabeth Coatsworth reprinted by permission of Coward-McCann Inc. From *Compass Rose* by Elizabeth Coatsworth, copyright 1929 by Coward-McCann, Inc. Copyright renewed © 1957 by Elizabeth Coatsworth.

Page 35: "What have I done to deserve all these kittens" by George Herriman. Copyright © 1934 by King Features Syndicate, Inc. Reprinted with special permission of King Features Syndicate, Inc.

Page 43: "The Happy Cat" from *The Complete Poems* by Randall Jarrell. Copyright © 1969 by Mrs. Randall Jarrell. Reprinted by permission of Farrar, Straus and Giroux, Inc.

Page 59: "Feline Felicity" by Charles Sheeler. Courtesy of The Fogg Art Museum, Harvard University, Cambridge, Massachusetts, Louise E. Bettens Fund.

Page 60: "The Great Cats and the Bears" by May Sarton is reprinted from *A Private Mythology, Poems* by May Sarton, by permission of W. W. Norton & Company, Inc. and by permission of Russell & Volkening as agents for the author. Copyright © 1966 by May Sarton.

Page 61: Untitled drawing by Edward Gorey. Reprinted by permission of Donadio and Ashworth Inc. Copyright © 1982 by Edward Gorey.

Page 64: "The Black Panther (from Leconte de Lisle)" by Richmond Lattimore. Copyright © 1951 by Alice Lattimore, from *Poems from Three Decades*, by Richmond Lattimore. Reprinted by permission of Alice Lattimore.

Page 67: "Wildcat" by Francis Colvin. Copyright © 1965 by Francis Colvin. Reprinted by permission of the author.

Page 68: "The Cat" by Philip Dacey. Copyright © 1971 by Philip Dacey, from *How I Escaped from the Labyrinth and Other Poems*, by Philip Dacey, Carnegie-Mellon U. Press, 1977. Reprinted by permission of the author.

Page 75: ". . . And the Mouse Police Never Sleeps" words and music by Ian Anderson. Copyright © 1978 Salamander and Sons Ltd./

Chrysalis Music Ltd. All rights in the U.S. and Canada administered by Chrysalis Music (ASCAP). International copyright secured. All rights reserved. Used by permission.

Page 77: Drawing by Chas. Addams; © 1975 The New Yorker Magazine, Inc.

Page 80: "Ailurophiles, Ailurophobes (excerpt)," from *A Celebration of Cats,* by Roger Caras. Copyright © 1987 by Roger A. Caras. Reprinted by permission of Simon & Schuster, Inc.

Page 94: "The Four-Eyed Cat" as told by N. Marchant. Reprinted from *Folktales of England,* by Katherine Briggs and Ruth Tongue. Copyright © 1965 by The University of Chicago Press. Reprinted by permission of The University of Chicago Press.

Page 106: "The Priceless Cats," from *The Priceless Cats and Other Italian Folk Stories,* by M. A. Jagendorf. Copyright © 1956 by M. A. Jagendorf and renewed 1984 by Andre Jagendorf. Reprinted by permission of Vanguard Press, a Division of Random House, Inc.

Page 112: "A Persian Tale" by Rose Fyleman. Excerpt(s) from *Forty Good-Morning Tales* by Rose Fyleman, copyright 1929 by Doubleday, a division of Bantam, Doubleday, Dell Publishing Group, Inc. Used by permission of the publisher and the Society of Authors as the literary representative of the Estate of Rose Fyleman.

Page 137: "Votive Stela" from *Egypt's Golden Age*. Reprinted by permission of Museum of Fine Arts Boston. Photo reproduced by permission of the Ashmolean Museum, Oxford.

Page 142: "Dr. Faustus to His Cats" by Anne Young. Copyright © 1951 by Saturday Review. Reprinted by permission of Omni Publications International.

Page 160: "The Heathens," excerpt from *The Heathens* by William Howells. Copyright 1948 by William Howells. Used by permission of Doubleday, a division of Bantam, Doubleday, Dell Publishing Group, Inc.

Page 161: "The Witch's Cat" adapted from "The Witch's Cat" by Marion Weinstein, published in *The Cat Catalog,* edited by Judy Fireman; © 1976 by Workman Publishing Company. Reprinted by permission of Workman Publishing. All rights reserved.

Page 165: Quote from "The Cat!" by Joseph Payne Brennan. Copyright © 1950 by Joseph Payne Brennan. Reprinted by permission of the author.

Page 168: "Cats are Queer Articles" as told to Eric Cross. Copyright by Devin-Adair, Publishers, Inc., Old Greenwich, Connecticut, 06870. Permission granted to reprint "Cats Are Queer Articles," from *The Tailor and the Antsy,* by Eric Cross, 1964.

Page 173: "Wait Till Martin Comes" recorded by W. E. Chilton. Reproduced by permission of the American Folklore Society from *Journal of American Folklore* 47: 186, 1934. Not for further reproduction.

Page 189: "Siva and Vishnu" by Melanie Schneider. Excerpt from *Cat People* by Bill Hayward, copyright 1978 by William Hayward, Jr. Used by permission of Doubleday, a division of Bantam, Doubleday, Dell Publishing Group, Inc.

Page 196: "When the Wind and the Rain" by Elizabeth Coatsworth reprinted by permission of Grosset & Dunlap, Inc. from *The Sparrow Bush* by Elizabeth Coatsworth. Copyright © 1966 by Grosset & Dunlap, Inc.

Page 196: "The cats are nervous when it is raining" by Edward Gorey. Reprinted by permission of Donadio and Ashworth Inc. Copyright © 1983, by Edward Gorey.

Page 200: "Studies of a Cat" by Beatrix Potter. From *The Art of Beatrix Potter,* by Enid and Leslie Linder, Frederick Warne and Co., Inc., NY, copyright 1955, p. 172. Reproduced by permission of Penguin Books Ltd.

Page 207: Quote by Paul Moore. Excerpt from *Cat People* by Bill Hayward, copyright 1978 by William Hayward, Jr. Used by permission of Doubleday, a division of Bantam, Doubleday, Dell Publishing Group, Inc.

Page 210: "In Connecticut There Are Cats" by Betty Lowry. Copyright © 1967 by Betty Lowry. Reprinted by permission of the author.

Page 214: "Cat on the Porch at Dusk" by Dorothy Harriman. Reprinted by permission from *The Christian Science Monitor,* copyright 1952 The Christian Science Publishing Society. All rights reserved.

Page 218: "Cat from the Night" by Hortense Roberta Roberts. Copyright © 1951 by Hortense Roberta Roberts. Reprinted by permission of the author.

Page 219: "Hearth" from *Animosities* by Peggy Bacon, copyright 1931 by Harcourt Brace Jovanovich, Inc. and renewed 1959 by Peggy Bacon. Reprinted by permission of Harcourt Brace Jovanovich, Inc.

Page 224: "Waiting for *It*", by May Swenson is reprinted by permission of the author, copyright 1957. Copyright renewed 1985 by May Swenson.

Page 225: "Ah How My Cat Benjamin" by Pauline M. Leet. Copyright © 1957 by Harper's Magazine. All rights reserved. Reprinted from the March issue by special permission.

Page 226: "On a Night of Snow" by Elizabeth Coatsworth. Copyright © by Elizabeth Coatsworth. Reproduced by permission of Margaret Coatsworth Beston.

Page 226: *Angora Cat* by Morris Hirshfield. (1937–39; dated on canvas 1937.) Oil on canvas, 22⅛ × 27¼". Collection, The Museum of Modern Art, New York; The Sidney and Harriet Janis Collection.

Page 228: "The Cat" by William Henry Davies. Copyright © 1963 by Jonathan Cape, Ltd. Reprint from *The Complete Poems of W. H. Davies* by permission of Wesleyan University Press and by permission of Jonathan Cape, Ltd.

Page 228: "Rose" by Mary Beth DiVito. Copyright © 1987 by Mary Beth DiVito. Reprinted by permission of the artist.

Page 229: "Villanelle for the Cat" Philip Dacey. Copyright © 1972 by Philip Dacey. Reprinted by permission of the author.

Index

Page references in italics indicate an illustration.

G

H

N

O

P

R